Tolley's
Capital Gains Tax
2006
Post-Budget Supplement

by

Kevin Walton BA (Hons)

Andrew Flint CTA

LexisNexis®
Tolley

Members of the LexisNexis Group worldwide

United Kingdom	LexisNexis Butterworths, a Division of Reed Elsevier (UK) Ltd, Halsbury House, 35 Chancery Lane, LONDON, WC2A 1EL, and RSH, 1–3 Baxter's Place, Leith Walk EDINBURGH EH1 3AF
Argentina	LexisNexis Argentina, BUENOS AIRES
Australia	LexisNexis Butterworths, CHATSWOOD, New South Wales
Austria	LexisNexis Verlag ARD Orac GmbH & Co KG, VIENNA
Benelux	LexisNexis Benelux, AMSTERDAM
Canada	LexisNexis Canada, MARKHAM, Ontario
Chile	LexisNexis Chile Ltda, SANTIAGO
China	LexisNexis China, BEIJING and SHANGHAI
France	LexisNexis SA, PARIS
Germany	LexisNexis Deutschland GmbH MUNSTER
Hong Kong	LexisNexis Hong Kong, HONG KONG
India	LexisNexis India, NEW DELHI
Italy	Giuffrè Editore, MILAN
Japan	LexisNexis Japan, TOKYO
Malaysia	Malayan Law Journal Sdn Bhd, KUALA LUMPUR
Mexico	LexisNexis Mexico, MEXICO
New Zealand	LexisNexis NZ ltd, WELLINGTON
Poland	Wydawnictwo Prawnicze LexisNexis Sp, WARSAW
Singapore	LexisNexis Singapore, SINGAPORE
South Africa	LexisNexis Butterworths, DURBAN
USA	LexisNexis, DAYTON, Ohio

© Reed Elsevier (UK) Ltd 2006
Published by LexisNexis Butterworths

A CIP Catalogue record for this book is available from the British Library.
ISBN 10: 0754529746
ISBN 13: 9780754529743

Printed and bound in Great Britain by Hobbs the PrintersLtd, Totton, Hampshire
Visit LexisNexis Butterworths at www.lexisnexis.co.uk

About This Supplement

This Supplement to Tolley's Capital Gains Tax 2005/06 gives details of changes in the law and practice of capital gains tax and corporation tax on chargeable gains from 2 July 2005 to **22 March 2006** (immediately before the Chancellor's Budget speech on that day). It lists the changes in the same order and under the same paragraph headings as the annual publication. Also included is a summary of the Chancellor's Budget proposals.

Each time Tolley's Capital Gains Tax 2005/06 is used, reference should be made to the material contained in this Supplement. The *Contents* give a list of all the chapters and paragraphs which have been updated.

TOLLEY

Contents

This Supplement contains amendments to the chapters and paragraphs of Tolley's Capital Gains Tax 2005/06 as listed below.

Contents

Contents

Contents

3 Anti-Avoidance

3.2 **Disclosure of tax avoidance schemes.** The following is added at the end of the paragraph immediately following the second set of bullet points on page 15.

'The Government has announced that from April 2006 the types of arrangements prescribed are to be extended to cover avoidance risks across all of income tax, capital gains tax and corporation tax. (Pre-Budget Report Press Notice PN03 5 December 2005).'

The following paragraph is added immediately before the paragraph headed 'Reference numbers allocated to arrangement' on page 18.

'The Government has announced that the time limit for disclosure of 'in-house' schemes is to be amended from April 2006, so that disclosure will have to be made within thirty days of implementation of the scheme. (Pre-Budget Report Press Notice PN03 5 December 2005).'

3.26 **Tax arbitrage.** The following paragraph is added at the end.

'**Clearance.** HMRC operate an advance clearance scheme for the above provisions and will give a decision wherever possible as to whether a notice will be issued in respect of proposed transactions. Sufficient information must be provided to enable HMRC to reach a view as to whether the provisions apply and procedures for clearance applications are set out in Annex C to the HMRC guidance to the provisions published on their web site on 2 August 2005. HMRC will consider themselves bound by any clearance given in accordance with those procedures. Clearance applications and any queries about the procedures should be sent to Andrew Hoar, HMRC (International CT), 100 Parliament Street, London SW1A 2BQ.'

3.27 The following is added.

'**Conversion of income to capital and capital losses used to create an income deduction.** New anti-avoidance provisions are to be introduced, applicable for corporation tax purposes only, to prevent the following types of avoidance schemes:

● schemes that convert an income profit into a capital gain, where allowable losses can then be set off against the gain; and

● schemes that use capital losses to cover a capital gain, and as part of the arrangements there is a related deduction from income profits.

Where the conditions set out in the provisions are met and HMRC issue a notice then the company will be denied the use of capital losses against the gain. There will be an explicit exclusion for the sale and leaseback of land and property, where the transactions are with third parties. HMRC will consider requests for informal advice about the application of the provisions to specific cases.

The provisions will apply to gains on disposals on or after 5 December 2005. For draft legislation and HMRC guidance see the Pre-Budget Report section of the HMRC web site (www.hmrc.gov.uk).'

4 Appeals

4.19 **Hearing and determination of proceedings.** The following is added at the beginning of the paragraph third from the end.

'In *McEwan v O'Donoghue (No 2) (Sp C 488), [2005] SSCD 681* the appellant was denied costs even though it was held that the Revenue had behaved wholly unreasonably, because the result of the appeal was that each party succeeded in roughly equal amounts.'

5   Assessments

5.2   **Discovery.** The last two paragraphs on page 66 and the first two paragraphs on page 67 are replaced with the following.

'Particularly in large or complex cases, the standard accounts information details and other information included in the personal tax return may not provide a means of disclosure adequate to avoid falling within (2)(ii) above. The submission of further information, including perhaps accounts, may be considered appropriate but will not necessarily provide protection against a discovery assessment beyond that arising from submission of the return alone. The reasonable expectation test (see (2)(ii) above) must be satisfied. Where voluminous information beyond the accounts and computations is sent with the return, HMRC do not accept that the test is satisfied if the information is so extensive that an officer could not reasonably be expected to be aware of the significance of particular information and the officer's attention has not been drawn to it by the taxpayer. HMRC will accept that for *TMA 1970, s 29* purposes documents submitted within a month of the return 'accompany' it (see (A) above) provided the return indicates that such documents have been or will be submitted. They will consider sympathetically a request that this condition be treated as satisfied where the time lag is longer than a month. (Revenue Tax Bulletin June 1996 pp 313–315; HMRC Statement of Practice 1/06).

In *Veltema v Langham CA, [2004] STC 544* a company director (V) was liable to income tax on the value of a house, and in his tax return he submitted a valuation of £100,000. After the deadline for making an enquiry into the return (see **53.8** RETURNS) had passed, the Revenue formed the opinion that the value of the house had been more than £100,000, and they subsequently issued a further assessment on the basis that the true value had been £145,000. V appealed, contending that the issue of a further assessment was not authorised by *TMA 1970, s 29*.The CA rejected this contention and upheld the assessment, holding that the assessment was not prohibited by *TMA 1970, s 29(5)* (i.e. (2)(ii) above). Prior to the enquiry deadline, the Revenue 'could not have been reasonably expected' to be aware that the valuation was inadequate. The CA observed that 'it would frustrate the aims of the self-assessment scheme, namely simplicity and early finality of assessment to tax, to interpret *s 29(5)* so as to introduce an obligation on tax inspectors to conduct an immediate and possibly time consuming scrutiny of self-assessment returns . . . when they do not disclose insufficiency, but only circumstances further investigation of which might or might not show it'. Furthermore, the definition of 'information made available' to the Revenue given above was exhaustive for the purpose of (2)(ii) above. The key to the scheme was that the inspector was precluded from making a discovery assessment under *section 29* only when the taxpayer or his representatives, in making an honest and accurate return, had clearly alerted him to the insufficiency of the assessment. He was not precluded from making an assessment where he might be able to obtain some other information, not normally part of his checks, that might put the sufficiency of the assessment in question.

Following the decision in this case the Revenue issued guidance on the amount of information which taxpayers need to provide to reduce or remove the risk of a discovery assessment in certain circumstances. That guidance has subsequently been formalised as HMRC Statement of Practice 1/06.

Where an entry in a return depends on the valuation of an asset, HMRC consider that most taxpayers who state in the additional information space at the end of the return that a valuation has been used, by whom it has been carried out, and that it was carried out by a named independent and suitably qualified valuer if that was the case, on the appropriate basis, will be able to rely on protection from a later discovery assessment after the enquiry period, provided those statements are true. Alternatively, in capital gains cases, completion of the entry in the capital gains pages indicating that a valuation has been made and inclusion of a copy of the valuation with the return will be sufficient to provide protection if the copy of the valuation includes all the information mentioned above. In some circumstances provision of the above information will not protect against a discovery assessment, particularly where other parties to the same transaction subsequently include a (different) valuation of the asset in their return.

Where a properly advised taxpayer adopts a different view of the law from that published as HMRC's view, to protect against a discovery assessment after the enquiry period HMRC consider that the return would have to indicate that a different view had been adopted. This might be done by an entry in the additional information space to the effect that HMRC guidance has not been followed on the issue or that no adjustment has been made to take account of it. In HMRC's view it is not necessary for the taxpayer to provide with the return enough information for the HMRC officer to be able to quantify any resulting under assessment of tax.

(Revenue Internet Statement 23 December 2004; HMRC Statement of Practice 1/06).'

The following paragraph is added before the penultimate paragraph.

'In *McEwan v Martin Ch D, [2005] STC 993*, a capital gains tax computation prepared by a professional adviser was held to constitute negligent conduct on the taxpayer's behalf, so that a discovery assessment could be made. The Revenue were entitled to assume that a professionally prepared tax computation was prepared properly, and the fact that they accepted a negligent computation at face value did not mean that it somehow ceased to be prepared negligently.'

6   Assets

6.6   **Milk quota.** A reference to *Foxton v HMRC (Sp C 485), [2005] SSCD 661* is added at the end of the third paragraph.

7   Assets held on 6 April 1965

7.1   The second paragraph (immediately following the list) is replaced by the following.

'**Married persons and civil partners.** The provisions relating to assets held on 6 April 1965 apply in relation to the disposal of an asset by one spouse or civil partner, who acquired it from the other spouse or civil partner in a year of assessment when they were living together, as if the other's acquisition or provision of the asset had been the acquisition etc. of the asset by the spouse or partner making the disposal. [*TCGA 1992, Sch 2 para 22; SI 2005 No 3229, Reg 124(b)*].'

7.3   **Elections.** The paragraph immediately preceding the example is replaced with the following.

'*Married persons and civil partners.* An election does not cover quoted securities which the holder acquired from his spouse or civil partner on a disposal after 19 March 1968 (or, again, after 31 March 1985) but such securities continue to be covered by an election which the transferor may have made. Where it is necessary to identify securities disposed of, earliest acquisitions are deemed to be disposed of first.'

A reference to *SI 2005 No 3229, Reg 124(a)* is added to the list of statutory references preceding the final paragraph.

9   Charities

9.7   **Gift aid donations by individuals.** A reference to *SI 2005 No 3229, Reg 104* is added to the list of statutory references three paragraphs from the end of the section headed 'The donor'.

A reference to *SI 2005 No 2790* is added to the list of references at the end of the section headed 'Qualifying donations'.

9.8   **Community amateur sports clubs.** The latest HMRC list of the names and addresses of registered clubs was published on 2 March 2006.

12   Companies

12.4   **Capital and income losses.** The following is added at the end of the first paragraph.

'Anti-avoidance rules are to be introduced, with effect for disposals on or after 5 December 2005, to ensure that capital losses can be created and used only as a result of genuine commercial transactions (Pre-Budget Report Press Notice PN03 5 December 2005). Draft legislation can be viewed on HMRC's web site (www.hmrc.gov.uk).'

The following is added at the end of the last paragraph.

'Note that these provisions are to be partially replaced by new anti-avoidance measures with effect from 5 December 2005. See the HMRC web site for draft legislation.'

12.27   **Restriction on set-off of pre-entry losses where a company joins a group.** The following paragraph is added at the end.

'These provisions are to be supplemented by new rules which will apply where tax avoidance is a main purpose of the acquisition of a company. The new rules will prevent the use of any capital losses (whether accruing before or after the change of ownership) on assets belonging to the company before the change to frank capital gains that arise on assets belonging to the new owners. The provisions will apply to tax advantages arising on or after 5 December 2005. For draft legislation and HMRC guidance see the Pre-Budget Report section on the HMRC web site (www.hmrc.gov.uk).'

12.38   **Restriction on set-off of losses against pre-entry gains where a company joins a group.** The following paragraphs are added at the end.

'*Proposed repeal and replacement.* The above provisions are to be repealed and replaced with a new targeted anti-avoidance rule. The new rule will apply where there is a change of ownership of a company and where the main purpose, or one of the main purposes of the arrangements, is the obtaining of a tax advantage. Where the new rule applies, any gains arising on assets owned by a company at the time of its change of ownership will only be capable of being franked by capital losses deriving from assets it held before the change. The acquiring company or group will not be able to offset its capital losses against capital gains arising in its new subsidiary.

The new provisions will apply to tax advantages arising on or after 5 December 2005. For draft legislation and HMRC guidance see the Pre-Budget Report section on the HMRC web site (www.hmrc.gov.uk).'

12.43   **Shares—acquisitions and disposals within short period.** The following paragraph is added at the end.

'The Government intends to repeal the above provisions with effect for disposals on or after 5 December 2005. It is considered that the provisions will be unnecessary following the introduction of the proposed restrictions on the use of capital losses to those deriving from genuine commercial transactions (see **12.2** above). See draft legislation in the Pre-Budget Report section of the HMRC web site (www.hmrc.gov.uk).'

12.50   **Definition of 'derivative contract'.** The text from the first list of statutory references to the end of the penultimate paragraph is amended to read as follows.

'[*FA 2002, Sch 26 paras 2, 12, 53(1)(2); SI 2004 No 2201, Arts 3, 13; SI 2004 No 3270, Art 3; SI 2005 No 3440, Arts 4, 6*].

Accounting tests etc. A relevant contract is *not* a derivative contract for the purposes of these provisions for an accounting period unless

- it is treated for accounting purposes as a derivative financial instrument in accordance with the relevant accounting standard (as defined) used by the company (or would be so treated if the company applied a relevant accounting standard to the relevant contract); or

- for periods of account beginning on or after 1 January 2005 and ending on or after 16 March 2005, it is not so treated solely because it does not meet the requirement in paragraph 9(d) of FRS 26 issued in December 2004 but is treated for accounting purposes as, or as forming part of, a financial asset or liability in accordance with the relevant accounting standard used by the company (or would be so treated if the company applied a relevant accounting standard to the relevant contract); or

- for periods of account beginning on or after 1 January 2005 and ending before 16 March 2005, it is a contract falling within *Sch 26 para 6* (contracts producing a guaranteed return — see (ii) below), *para 7* (contracts with a guaranteed amount payable on maturity — see (iii) below) or *para 8* (contracts held by company to provide insurance benefits — see (iv) below); or

- for periods of account beginning before 1 January 2005, it is a contract falling within *Sch 26 para 6* or *para 7* and it is treated for accounting purposes as a financial asset in accordance with the relevant accounting standard (as defined) (or would be so treated if the company applied that standard to the relevant contract); or

- its 'underlying subject matter' (see below) is commodities; or

- it is a contract for differences (see above) and its underlying subject matter is

  - for contracts entered into on or after 1 August 2004 in an accounting period ending after 16 September 2004, land (wherever situated);

  - for contracts entered into on or after 1 August 2004 in an accounting period ending after 16 September 2004, tangible movable property other than commodities which are tangible assets;

  - intangible fixed assets (see **12.55** below);

  - weather conditions; or

  - creditworthiness.

[*FA 2002, Sch 26 paras 3, 12(11); SI 2004 No 2201, Arts 1, 4, 13(3); SI 2005 Nos 646, Art 3, 2082, Art 4*].

Contracts excluded by virtue of their underlying subject matter. Subject to the qualifications below, a relevant contract is not a derivative contract for the purposes of these provisions if its underlying subject matter consists wholly of one or more types of 'excluded property'.

For periods of account beginning on or after 1 January 2005 and ending on or after 16 March 2005, the following are 'excluded property':

(A)   intangible fixed assets (see **12.55** below) (but these are not excluded if the relevant contract is a contract for differences);

(B)   shares in a company (as defined);

(C)   rights of a unit holder under a unit trust scheme.

Exclusions (B) and (C) above apply only where, broadly, the contract is entered into for non-trading purposes or by a life assurance company or mutual trading company or where the contract is part of a hedging relationship.

Previously, the following were '*excluded property*':

(*a*)   for contracts entered into before 1 August 2004 and for contracts entered into on or after that date in accounting periods ending before 17 September 2004, land (whether in the UK or elsewhere);

(*b*)   for contracts entered into before 1 August 2004 and for contracts entered into on or after that date in accounting periods ending before 17 September 2004, tangible movable property, other than commodities which are tangible assets;

(*c*)   intangible fixed assets (but not if the relevant contract is a contract for differences);

(*d*)   shares in a company;

(*e*)   rights of a unit holder under a unit trust scheme;

(*f*)   for periods of account beginning before 1 January 2005, assets representing loan relationships which are within *FA 1996, s 92* or *s 93* (convertible or asset-linked securities — see **37.8** LOAN RELATIONSHIPS OF COMPANIES).

The underlying subject matter of a relevant contract is *treated* as consisting wholly of one or more of the above in certain circumstances if it consists partly of such property and partly of other property, where the latter is subordinate to the former or of small value compared with the whole. See also **12.53** below for the splitting of a contract into two notional contracts (applicable only to futures and options).

The '*underlying subject matter*' of a relevant contract is

●   (in the case of an option) the property which would fall to be delivered if the option were exercised; or, where such property is itself a derivative contract, the underlying subject matter of that contract;

●   (in the case of a future) the property which, if the future were to run to delivery, would fall to be delivered at the date and price agreed when the contract is made; or, where such property is itself a derivative contract, the underlying subject matter of that contract;

●   (in the case of a contract for differences), where the contract relates to fluctuations in the value or price of property described in the contract, the property so described; or, where the contract designates an index or factor, the matter by reference to which the index or factor is determined (and in particular, underlying subject matter may include interest rates, weather conditions or creditworthiness, but the use of interest rates to establish the amount of a payment whose due date may vary does not make those rates the underlying subject matter of the contract).

For contracts entered into on or after 1 August 2004 in an accounting period ending on or after 17 September 2004, where the underlying subject matter of a relevant contract consists of or includes income from shares in a company or rights of a unit trust holder or unit trust scheme (or, for periods of account beginning before 1 January 2005 and ending before 16 March 2005, land), the underlying subject matter is not to be treated, by reason only of that income, as being such shares or rights (or land).

[*FA 2002, Sch 26 paras 4, 9, 11, 12; SI 2004 No 2201, Arts 5, 11, 12; SI 2005 No 646, Arts 1, 4, ; SI 2005 No 2082, Arts 5, 8; SI 2005 No 2440, Arts 5, 6*].

Exclusions (*d*)–(*f*) above do not apply where:

(i)   the relevant contract is entered into or acquired by the company for the purposes of a trade carried on by it; or

(ii)   the relevant contract is designed, either by itself or together with certain 'associated transactions' (as defined), to produce a 'guaranteed return' (as defined); or

(iii)   the relevant contract is designed, either by itself or together with certain 'associated transactions' (as defined), to secure that the amount payable on maturity does not fall below a guaranteed amount (defined as, broadly, 80% of the consideration payable for entering into, or acquiring, the contract or associated transactions); or

(iv)   the company is carrying on long-term insurance business and the relevant contract is designed to provide certain benefits under life insurance or capital redemption policies.

For periods of account beginning on or after 1 January 2005 and ending before 16 March 2005, exclusion (*d*) above does not apply where the contract of a company is a deemed relevant contract to which the company is treated as party under the above embedded derivatives rules or under the embedded derivatives rules of *FA 1996, s 94A(2)* (see **37.5** LOAN RELATIONSHIPS OF COMPANIES).

[*FA 2002, Sch 26 paras 5–8, 10; SI 2004 No 2201, Arts 6–10; SI 2004 No 3270, Art 4; SI 2005 No 646, Arts 1, 6, 8*].

For periods of account beginning before 1 January 2005 and ending before 16 March 2005, a company may elect to treat a contract within (iii) above as divided on a just and reasonable basis into two separate contracts, one a creditor loan relationship (see **37.3** LOAN RELATIONSHIPS OF COMPANIES) which is a 'relevant zero coupon bond' (as defined) and the other an option to which (ii)–(iv) above do not apply and which may therefore be excluded property. [*FA 2002, Sch 26 para 48; FA 2004, Sch 10 para 64; SI 2005 No 646, Arts 1, 20*].

Transitional provisions for contracts becoming derivative contracts. The following provisions apply where a company is a party to a relevant contract immediately before and immediately after 3 p.m. on 16 March 2005, and the contract becomes a derivative contract immediately after that time having previously been a 'chargeable asset' (i.e. an asset in respect of which a gain on disposal would be a chargeable gain). When the company ceases to be a party to the contract it has to bring into account, for the accounting period in which it so ceases, the amount of any chargeable gain or allowable loss that would have accrued to the company on a disposal of the asset immediately before 3 p.m. on 16 March 2005 for a consideration equal to the value given to the contract in the company accounts at the end of the accounting period immediately before its first new period. [*FA 2002, Sch 26 para 4A; SI 2005 No 646, Art 5*].

Further transitional provisions apply where a company is party to a relevant contract both immediately before and on 28 July 2005 and the contract was a chargeable asset and not a derivative contract immediately before that date but would have been a derivative contract on that date had an accounting period of the company begun on that date. The contract is treated as a derivative contract entered into by the company on 28 July 2005 for a consideration equal to the fair value of the contract on that date. When the company ceases to be a party to the contract it has to bring into account, for the accounting period in which it so ceases, the amount of any chargeable gain or allowable loss that would have accrued to the company on a disposal, at fair value, of the contract immediately before 28 July 2005.

A relevant contract to which a company becomes a party on or after 28 July 2005 is treated in the hands of the company as a derivative contract if, on the date on which the company so becomes a party to it, it is a chargeable asset but would be a derivative contract if an accounting period began on that date.

[*FA 2002, Sch 26 paras 4B, 4C; SI 2005 No 2082, Art 6*].'

12   Companies

12.51   **Derivative contracts taxed on a chargeable gains basis.** The two paragraphs immediately following list (*a*) to (*c*) are replaced by the following.

'As regards (*a*) and (*c*) above, chargeable gains treatment does not apply where the company is an authorised unit trust, an investment trust, an open-ended investment company or a venture capital trust. Nor, as regards (*a*) above, does it apply in the case of an embedded derivative which is an exactly tracking contract for differences whose underlying subject matter is land within (*b*) above or (for periods of account beginning on or after 1 January 2005 and ending on or after 16 March 2005) where *FA 2002, Sch 26 para 45K* (issuers of securities with embedded derivatives — deemed contracts for differences; see **12.52** below) applies to the contract. Where the underlying subject matter includes income, this is ignored in determining the underlying subject matter of the contract, where it is subordinate to the land or property in question, or small in value in comparison with the underlying subject matter of the contract as a whole.

[*FA 2002, Sch 26 paras 45A, 45C, 45D((2)(a)(3), 45F(2)(a)(3), 45G(1A)(1B); SI 2004 No 2201, Arts 1, 15; SI 2004 No 3270, Art 8; SI 2005 No 2082, Art 12; SI 2005 No 3440, Art 8*].'

A reference to *SI 2005 No 2082, Arts 13–15* is added to the list of statutory references three paragraphs from the end of page 180.

The following is added at the end.

'*Terminal exercise of options.* For periods of account beginning on or after 1 January 2005 and ending on or after 1 August 2005 there are provisions dealing with the chargeable gains consequences of the exercise or, for accounting periods ending on or after 31 December 2005, disposal of rights to acquire shares comprised in a derivative contract which is, or is treated as, an option.

Where the contract is an embedded derivative within (i) above the following applies.

(A)   In computing any chargeable gain accruing on a disposal of the asset representing the creditor relationship associated with the embedded derivative, the acquisition cost is increased by the amount by which G (see below) exceeds L or, where L exceeds G, is reduced by the excess.

(B)   In computing any chargeable gain accruing on a disposal of all the shares acquired in exercising the rights where, for accounting periods ending on or after 31 December 2005, the acquisition was in circumstances such that no disposal was deemed to arise by virtue of *TCGA 1992, s 127* (reorganisation of share capital — see **57.1** SHARES AND SECURITIES), the acquisition cost is increased by the amount by which G (see below) exceeds L or, where L exceeds G, is reduced by the excess. In the case of a part disposal of the shares, the part disposal apportionment rule at **16.6** DISPOSAL applies accordingly.

In either case, where L exceeds G and the excess is greater than the acquisition cost, any remaining amount is added to the disposal consideration.

For these purposes, G is the sum of the 'initial carrying value' of the contract and any chargeable gains accruing under *FA 2002, Sch 26 para 45A* above in respect of the contract for the accounting period in which the disposal is made and any previous accounting periods so far as they are referable, on a just and reasonable apportionment, to the shares. L is the sum of any allowable losses accruing for those accounting periods so far as they are so referable. The '*initial carrying value*' of a contract is the amount treated in accordance with *FA 1996, s 94A(2)* as the carrying value of the contract at the time the company became party to the loan relationship.

Where the contract is not an embedded derivative, in computing any chargeable gain accruing on a disposal of all the shares acquired in exercising the rights, the acquisition cost is increased by the amount by which X (see below) exceeds Y or, where Y exceeds X, is reduced by the excess and, in the case of a part disposal of the shares, the part disposal apportionment rule at **16.6** DISPOSAL applies accordingly. Where Y exceeds X and the excess is greater than the acquisition cost, any remaining amount is added to the disposal consideration.

For this purpose, X is the sum of any credits brought into account as trading receipts in respect of the derivative contract for the accounting period in which the disposal is made and any previous accounting periods so far as they are referable, on a just and reasonable apportionment, to the shares. Y is the sum of any debits so brought into account for those accounting periods so far as they are so referable.

[*FA 2002, Sch 26 paras 45H, 45HA; SI 2005 No 2082, Arts 1, 17; SI 2005 No 3440, Arts 9, 10*].'

12.52   The text is replaced by the following.

'*Issuers of securities with embedded derivatives — deemed options.* There are also provisions dealing with certain embedded derivatives on a chargeable gains basis where the loan relationship in which the derivative is embedded is a *debtor* relationship of the company. Subject to further conditions, the following provisions apply for periods of account beginning on or after 1 January 2005 to embedded derivatives which are deemed to be options and whose underlying subject matter is shares.

Where the provisions apply, non-trading and, for periods of account ending on or after 17 August 2005, trading debits and credits are not brought into account under the loan relationship rules as outlined at **12.49** above. Instead, the following applies.

(*a*)   Where the option is exercised and shares are issued or transferred in fulfilment of the obligations under the option (the '*relevant disposal*'), *TCGA 1992, s 144(2)* (see **16.10** DISPOSAL) applies to the relevant disposal as if the 'initial carrying value' was the consideration for the grant of the option. For periods of account ending on or after 17 August 2005, the market value rule at *TCGA 1992, s 17(1)* (see **39.1** MARKET VALUE) is disapplied.

(*b*)   Where the option is exercised, there is no relevant disposal and an amount is paid in fulfilment of the obligations under the option, a chargeable gain is treated as accruing to the company equal to the excess of the initial carrying value over the amount paid by the debtor in fulfilment of the obligation or, if a single amount is paid in fulfilment of the obligations under the debtor relationship, the part of the amount falling for accounting purposes to be treated as the amount relating to the option. For periods of account ending before 17 August 2005, the gain is the excess of the initial carrying value over the amount paid in fulfilment of the obligation reduced by the aggregate of the initial carrying value and the carrying amount of the host contract at the time the company became party to the loan relationship. In either case, an allowable loss will accrue if the initial carrying value is less than the latter amount.

(*c*)   Where the debtor relationship comes to an end without the option having been exercised, the company is treated for the purposes of corporation tax on chargeable gains as having disposed of the option for an amount equal to the initial carrying value. For periods of account ending on or after 17 August 2005, the acquisition cost of the option is deemed to be so much of the amount paid by the company in consideration for it ceasing to be a party to the debtor relationship as falls to be treated for accounting purposes as the amount relating to the option.

If the company was a party to the debtor relationship immediately before its first accounting period beginning on or after 1 January 2005, (*a*) and (*c*) above do not apply and for the purposes of (*b*) above the initial carrying value is taken to be nil.

For these purposes, the '*initial carrying value*' means the amount treated in accordance with *FA 1996, s 94A(2)* as the carrying value of the option at the time the company became party to the loan relationship.

[*FA 2002, Sch 26 para 45J; SI 2004 No 3270, Art 10; SI 2005 No 646, Art 16; SI 2005 No 2082, Arts 1, 18; SI 2005 No 3440, Art 11*].

Issuers of securities with embedded derivatives — equity instruments. Subject to further conditions, the following applies for periods of account beginning on or after 1 January 2005 and ending on or after 16 March 2005 where a debtor relationship is divided under the embedded derivatives provisions between the loan relationship and an equity instrument, such that the equity instrument is a relevant contract treated as an option but is not a derivative contract. Where the company pays an amount to the person who is party to the loan relationship as creditor in discharge of any obligations under the relationship an allowable loss is treated as accruing to the extent that RA exceeds E. For this purpose, RA is the amount so paid less so much of that amount as is treated for accounting purposes as paid in discharge of the liabilities under the loan relationship element, and E is the amount treated in accordance with *FA 1996, s 94A(2)* as the carrying value of the relevant contract at the time the company became party to the loan relationship. These provisions do not apply where the liability representing the debtor relationship was owed by the company immediately before its first accounting period beginning on or after 1 January 2005. [*FA 2002, Sch 26 para 45JA; SI 2005 No 2082, Arts 1, 19*].

Issuers of securities with embedded derivatives — deemed contracts for difference. Subject to further conditions, the following applies for periods of account beginning on or after 1 January 2005 where a debtor relationship is divided under the embedded derivatives provisions such that the relevant contract to which the company is treated as being party is a derivative contract whose underlying subject matter is land or shares and which is a contract for differences (other than one falling within *FA 2002, Sch 26 para 45J* above). The contract must be an exactly tracking contract (as defined) or, for periods of account ending on or after 17 August 2005, must be excluded from being such a contract only by a specific condition (see *FA 2002, Sch 26 para 45K(1)(d)*).

Non-trading and, for periods of account ending on or after 17 August 2005, trading debits and credits are not brought into account under the loan relationship rules as outlined at **12.49** above. For periods of account ending on or after 17 August 2005, where the debtor relationship comes to an end and an amount is paid to discharge all of the company's obligations (the '*discharge amount*'), a chargeable gain or allowable loss is treated as accruing, calculated on the assumption that the derivative contract is an asset of the company, that there is a disposal of that asset at the time the relationship comes to an end, that the consideration for the disposal is equal to the amount of the proceeds of issue of the security representing the relationship, and that the cost of the asset is the discharge amount.

For periods of account ending on or after 17 August 2005, these provisions do not apply where the liability representing the debtor relationship was owed by the company immediately before its first accounting period beginning on or after 1 January 2005.

[*FA 2002, Sch 26 para 45K; SI 2005 No 2082, Arts 1, 20*].'

12.53   **Miscellaneous rules with potential chargeable gains consequences.** The final paragraph is replaced by the following.

'*Treasury power to amend provisions.* Following *FA 2004*, the Treasury may amend *FA 2002, Sch 26 Pt 9* (including *paras 44–47* above and the provisions at **12.50–12.52** above) by order. [*FA 2002, Sch 26 para 13; FA 2004, s 49, Sch 9 para 2*]. A number of such orders have been made, and these are covered above and at **12.50–12.52** above.'

13   Connected Persons

A reference to *SI 2005 No 3229, Regs 100, 121* is added to the list of statutory references at the head of the chapter.

13.1   The text is replaced by the following.

'An **individual** is connected with his spouse or civil partner, any 'relative' (see **13.7** below) of himself or of his spouse or civil partner, and with the spouse or civil partner of any such relative. It appears that a widow or widower is no longer a spouse (*Vestey's Exors and Vestey v CIR HL 1949, 31 TC 1*). Spouses divorced by decree nisi remain connected persons until the divorce is made absolute (*Aspden v Hildesley Ch D 1981, 55 TC 609*).'

13.3   The text is replaced by the following.

'**Partners** are connected with each other and with each other's spouses (see **13.1** above), civil partners and relatives (see **13.7** below), except in connection with acquisitions and disposals of partnership assets made pursuant to *bona fide* commercial arrangements. See also **13.5** below.'

14   Corporate Venturing Scheme

14.5   **Qualifying investing company.** A reference to *SI 2005 No 3229, Reg 132* is added at the end of the section headed '"No control" requirement'.

14.6   **Qualifying issuing company.** The section headed 'Individual-owners requirement' is replaced by the following.

'**Individual-owners requirement.** Throughout the qualification period, at least **20%** of the issued ordinary share capital of the issuing company must be beneficially owned by one or more 'independent individuals'. An '*independent individual*' is one who is not, at any time during the qualification period when he holds ordinary shares in the issuing company, a director or employee of the investing company or of any company connected with it (within *ICTA 1988, s 839* — see **13** CONNECTED PERSONS), or a relative (i.e. husband, wife, civil partner, forebear or issue) of such a director or employee. Where an independent individual owned shares immediately prior to his death, they are treated for these purposes as continuing to be owned by an independent individual until they cease to form part of the deceased's estate. [*FA 2000, Sch 15 paras 18, 102(3); SI 2005 No 3229, Reg 132*].'

16   Disposal

16.5   **Non-allowable expenditure.** The following paragraph is added at the end.

'In *Smallwood v HMRC Sp C 2005 (Sp C 509), [2006] SSCD 12, TCGA 1992, s 41* was held not to restrict a loss on units in an enterprise zone unit trust where the trustees of the unit trust had used the funds subscribed for the units to acquire land and buildings, in respect of which the taxpayer had been credited with capital allowances. The Special Commissioner held that capital allowances had not been made in respect of the taxpayer's expenditure in subscribing for the units. It was the trustees' expenditure that had resulted in capital allowances for the taxpayer.'

17   Double Tax Relief

17.2   **Double tax agreements.** The following are added to the list.

Chile (2003/3200 — applies in UK from 1 April 2005 for corporation tax and from 6 April 2005 for capital gains tax).

Georgia (2004/3325 — applies in UK from 1 April 2006 for corporation tax and from 6 April 2006 for capital gains tax).

The following is added to the Notes under Agreements not yet in force.

'A new agreement was signed with Botswana on 9 September 2005. A new agreement was signed with Japan on 2 February 2006.'

17.9   **Special withholding tax.** A reference is added in the fourth paragraph to the agreement signed with Gibraltar (see HMRC Internet Statement, 21 December 2005).

18   Employee Share Schemes

18.22   **Special rules where replacement asset is a dwelling-house.** The final three paragraphs are replaced by the following.

'The said rules apply where the property later comes within the private residence exemption (see **47** PRIVATE RESIDENCES) (or would do if it were disposed of) by reference to the claimant or the claimant's spouse or civil partner (whether as an individual taxpayer or as a person entitled to occupy the property under the terms of a settlement).

If there is a time after the acquisition and *before* the making of the rollover relief claim when the dwelling-house etc. would fall within the private residence exemption, it is treated as if it had not been a chargeable asset in relation to the claimant immediately after the acquisition, with the result that the rollover relief claim fails. If, instead, there is a time *after* the making of the rollover relief claim when the dwelling-house etc. would fall within the private residence exemption, it is similarly treated, but in this case the gain rolled over is treated as not having accrued until that time (or until the earliest of such times if there is more than one).

Similar rules apply where the replacement asset is an option to acquire (or to acquire an interest in) a dwelling-house etc., and the option is exercised.

[*TCGA 1992, Sch 7C para 6; SI 2005 No 3229, Reg 129*].'

18.26   **Save as you earn (SAYE) share option schemes.** In the third paragraph from the end, the references to Revenue leaflets IR 97 and IR 98 are removed (those leaflets having been withdrawn).

18.27   **Company share option plan (CSOP) schemes.** In the paragraph immediately before the heading 'Capital gains tax', the references to Revenue leaflets IR 101 and IR 102 are removed (those leaflets having been withdrawn).

18.29   **Approved profit sharing schemes.** In the final paragraph, the references to Revenue leaflets IR 95 and 96 are removed (that leaflet having been withdrawn).

18.36   **Dwelling-houses: special provisions.** The first paragraph is amended to read as follows.

'As regards **18.32**(*d*) above, a replacement asset which is a dwelling-house (or part thereof) or land is not treated (where it would otherwise be so treated) as being a chargeable asset in relation to the claimant immediately after the asset's acquisition if on a disposal of it (or an interest in it) at some time in the period from its acquisition to the time a claim is made under *TCGA 1992, s 229(1)* or *(3)* (see **18.32** above), the PRIVATE RESIDENCES **(47.1)** exemption of *TCGA 1992, s 222(1)* would apply to the asset (or interest in it) and the 'individual' (which includes references to a person entitled to occupy the dwelling-house etc. under the terms of a settlement; see **47.5** PRIVATE RESIDENCES) mentioned in *TCGA 1992, s 222(1)* would be the claimant or his spouse or civil partner.'

A reference to *SI 2005 No 3229, Reg 119* is added to the final paragraph.

19 Enterprise Investment Scheme

19.2 **Income tax relief.** The first five sentences of the section headed 'Withdrawal of relief on disposal' are replaced by the following.

'Where the investor disposes of EIS shares before the end of the 'relevant period' (as in **19.3**(*a*) below), EIS income tax relief given falls to be withdrawn. This does not apply on a transfer to the investor's spouse or civil partner made at a time they are living together; the transferee stands in the shoes of the transferor as regards any subsequent disposal. If a disposal is not made by way of bargain at arm's length, the relief is fully withdrawn in all cases. Otherwise, the relief given is fully withdrawn unless it is greater than tax at the lower rate (for the tax year for which the relief was given) on the amount or value of the consideration received on disposal, in which case only the lower amount is withdrawn. [*ICTA 1988, s 299(1)–(3), s 304; FA 1994, Sch 15 paras 12, 18; FA 1998, s 74, Sch 13 para 12(1)(2)(8), para 16; SI 2005 No 3229, Reg 65].*'

19.8 **Capital gains tax.** A reference to *SI 2005 No 3229, Reg 110* is added immediately after the first bullet point list.

19.10 **Reinvestment into EIS shares issued after 5 April 1998.** The text from the heading 'Deferred gain becoming chargeable' down to the beginning of the example is replaced by the following.

'The deferred gain will become chargeable upon the occurrence of, *and at the time of*, any of the chargeable events listed below. The amount of the gain accruing at the time of the chargeable event is equal to so much of the deferred gain as is attributable to the EIS shares in relation to which the chargeable event occurs. For these purposes, a proportionate part of the net deferred gain (i.e. the deferred gain less any amount brought into charge on an earlier part disposal) is attributed to each of the 'relevant shares' held, immediately before the chargeable event, by the investor or by a person who acquired them from the investor on a transfer between spouses or civil partners within *TCGA 1992, s 58*. The '*relevant shares*' are the shares acquired in making the qualifying investment and, in a case where the original gain accrued at a later time than the making of the qualifying investment, still held at that time. They also include any bonus shares issued in respect of the relevant shares and of the same class and carrying the same rights. These rules were modified by *FA 1999, Sch 8* and are described here in their modified form. The modifications affect part disposals (see the *Example* below) and give statutory effect in relation to shares issued after 5 April 1999 to the Revenue's interpretation of the previous rules (Treasury Explanatory Notes to Finance Bill 1999). The said chargeable events are as follows.

(i) The investor disposes of the EIS shares otherwise than by way of a transfer between spouses or civil partners to which *TCGA 1992, s 58* applies.

(ii) Subsequent to a transfer within *TCGA 1992, s 58*, the shares are disposed of by the investor's spouse or civil partner (otherwise than by way of transfer back to the investor).

(iii) Within the designated period (see below), the investor becomes neither resident nor ordinarily resident in the UK.

(iv) Within the designated period (see below), the investor's spouse or civil partner, having acquired the shares by way of transfer within *TCGA 1992, s 58*, becomes neither resident nor ordinarily resident in the UK.

(v) The shares cease to be eligible shares or are treated as so ceasing (see below).

For these purposes, the designated period is

- (for shares issued after 5 April 2000) the period ending immediately before the third anniversary of the date of issue of the shares or, if later and where relevant, the third anniversary of the date of commencement of the intended trade referred to in **19.6**(*a*) above; or

- (for shares issued before 6 April 2000) the five years beginning with the issue of the shares.

In the case of (iii) or (iv) above (non-residence), the deferred gain does not become chargeable where the investor (or, where applicable, spouse or civil partner) becomes neither resident nor ordinarily resident through temporary working outside the UK and again becomes resident or ordinarily resident within three years of that event, without having disposed of any of the relevant shares in the meantime in circumstances such that a chargeable event would have occurred had he been UK resident. No assessment is to be made until it is clear that the person concerned will not regain UK resident status within the three-year period.

EIS shares are *treated* as ceasing to be eligible shares (in which case a chargeable event occurs under (v) above) in any of the following circumstances (and see also the further provisions in **19.12** below).

(1)   The condition at (*b*) above (qualifying company) ceases to be satisfied in consequence of an event occurring after the issue of the shares: the shares cease to be eligible shares at the time of that event. The Revenue have confirmed that the company is required to retain its qualifying status only for the duration of the 'relevant period' (as defined in **19.6** above), so no chargeable event can occur under this heading by reason of anything happening beyond the end of that period (*Taxation 18 February 1999 p 486*).

(2)   The condition at (*e*) above (compliance with *ICTA 1988, s 289(1A)*) ceases to be satisfied in consequence of an event occurring after the issue of the shares: the shares cease to be eligible shares at the time of that event.

(3)   The condition at (*g*) above (money raised to be used for purpose of qualifying business activity within a specified time period) is not satisfied and the deferral claim was made before the end of the time period of 12 or 24 months (whichever is relevant): the shares cease to be eligible shares at the end of that time period. (If the deferral claim has not been made by then, or if the condition at (*f*) above is not satisfied at all, the shares are treated as never having been eligible shares.)

Death. The deferred gain does not become chargeable on the death of the investor (or, where applicable, spouse or civil partner) or on the occurrence after death of any event which would otherwise have been a chargeable event.

Identification rules. In determining whether any shares disposed of after 5 April 1998 are shares to which deferral relief is attributable (see **19.9** above), the normal identification rules (see **58.2** SHARES AND SECURITIES—IDENTIFICATION RULES) are disapplied and, instead, the same rules as in **19.8** above apply (broadly, first in/first out but with special rules where shares acquired on the same day fall into different specified categories — see examples at HMRC Venture Capital Schemes Manual VCM 38290).

Where at the time of the chargeable event, any of the relevant shares are regarded under capital gains tax legislation as represented by assets which consist of or include assets other than such shares, the deferred gain attributable to those shares is to be apportioned between those assets on a just and reasonable basis. As between different assets regarded as representing the same shares, the identification of those assets follows the same identification rules as for shares.

Persons chargeable. The chargeable gain is treated as accruing, depending on which type of chargeable event occurs, to

- the individual who makes the disposal;
- the individual who becomes non-resident;
- the individual who holds the shares in question when they cease (or are treated as ceasing) to be eligible shares.

Where the last category applies and some of the shares are held by the investor and some by a person who acquired them from the investor by way of transfer between spouses or civil partners within *TCGA 1992, s 58*, the gain is computed separately as regards each individual without reference to the shares held by the other.

[*TCGA 1992, ss 105A(4)(7)(8), 150C, Sch 5B paras 1–6, 19; FA 1995, s 67, Sch 13 para 4(3)(4); FA 1998, s 74, Sch 13 paras 26–33, 36, Sch 27 Pt III(14); FA 1999, s 73, Sch 8; FA 2000, Sch 17 para 7(2)(3), para 8; FA 2001, Sch 15 paras 26–29, 37, 40, Sch 33 Pt II(3); FA 2002, s 50; FA 2004, s 93, Sch 18 paras 13, 14, 20(1)(b), 21, Sch 19 para 6, Sch 42 Pt 2(12); SI 2005 No 3229, Reg 127*].

See the further provisions at **19.12** below.'

19.12 **Reinvestment into EIS shares issued after 5 April 1998 — further provisions.** References to *SI 2005 No 3229, Reg 127* are added to the statutory references at the end of (1), (2) and (3).

In the section in (2) headed 'Put and call options', in the penultimate sentence, the words 'or civil partner' are inserted after 'subscriber spouse'.

20 Exemptions and Reliefs

20.3 **Annuities and annual payments.** The following is added at the end of the first paragraph.

'The Government intends to amend these provisions, with effect for disposals on or after 5 December 2005, to prevent the creation of allowable losses on certain non-deferred annuities. For draft legislation and explanatory notes see the Pre-Budget Report section of the HMRC web site (www.hmrc.gov.uk).'

20.10 **Insurance policies.** The following is added at the end of the first paragraph.

'The Government intends to amend these provisions, with effect for disposals on or after 5 December 2005, to block avoidance schemes purporting to create allowable losses on capital redemption policies. For draft legislation and explanatory notes see the Pre-Budget Report section of the HMRC web site (www.hmrc.gov.uk).'

20.15 **Ships and other assets within the tonnage tax regime.** Reference is made to *SI 2006 No 333* which disapplies the requirement for new ships entering tonnage tax to be registered in the EU for financial year 2006.

20.19 **Business expansion scheme.** The third paragraph from the end of page 329 is replaced by the following.

'In computing gains or losses arising on an individual's disposal of shares **issued before 19 March 1986** in respect of which BES relief has been given and not withdrawn, that relief is disregarded *except* to the extent that an unindexed loss would otherwise accrue, in which case the deductible expenditure is reduced by the smaller of the BES relief given (and not withdrawn) and the amount of the loss. [*TCGA 1992, s 150(3)*]. It was held in *Quinn v Cooper Ch D 1998, 71 TC 44* that indexation allowance should be based on the reduced cost. *Section 150(3)* does not apply to disposals within *TCGA 1992, s 58(1)* (see **40.3** MARRIED PERSONS AND CIVIL PARTNERS) but will apply on a subsequent disposal to a third party by the transferee. In determining whether any sums are excluded under *TCGA 1992, s 39(1)(2)*

20   Exemptions and Reliefs

(exclusion of expenditure allowable against income — see **16.5** DISPOSAL), the existence of any relief given and not withdrawn is ignored.'

In the list of statutory references on page 330, a reference to *SI 2005 No 3229, Reg 109* is added.

20.21   **Child trust funds.** The first sentence of the second paragraph is replaced by the following.

'No tax is chargeable in respect of interest, dividends, distributions, gains or (from 27 December 2005) alternative financial arrangement return on account investments.'

In the list of statutory references at the end, a reference to *SI 2005 No 3349* is added.

20.28   **Individual savings accounts (ISAs).** The text from the beginning down to and including the fourth paragraph on page 334 is replaced by the following.

'ISAs are available **after 5 April 1999** to individuals over 18 (though see below) who are both resident and ordinarily resident in the UK and will continue to be available for a minimum of ten years. The accounts can be made up of cash, stocks and shares and, before 6 April 2005, life insurance (see below). They were introduced as a replacement for PEPs and TESSAs, although see **20.30** below as regards PEPs already in existence at the end of 1998/99 and note that neither the value of PEP holdings nor any capital transferred to an ISA from a TESSA (tax-exempt special savings account) will affect the amount which can be subscribed to an ISA. Investors can subscribe up to £7,000 to an ISA in each tax year up to and including 2009/10, of which a maximum of £3,000 can go into cash and, for 2004/05 and earlier years, £1,000 into life insurance. See further details below. After 5 April 2001, the availability of cash ISAs is extended to 16 and 17-year olds. There is no statutory lock-in, minimum subscription, minimum holding period or lifetime subscription limit. Withdrawals may be made at any time without loss of tax relief but not so as to allow further subscriptions in breach of the annual maximum.

Interest and dividends are free of income tax (and a 10% tax credit is payable on dividends received from UK equities before 6 April 2004). Gains arising from assets held within an ISA are not chargeable gains for CGT purposes (and losses are not allowable).

[*TCGA 1992, s 151; ICTA 1988, ss 333, 333A; FA 1998, ss 75, 76, Sch 27 Pt III(15); ITTOIA 2005, ss 694–701, Sch 1 paras 141, 436, 503*].

The Individual Savings Account Regulations 1998 (*SI 1998 No 1870* as amended) provide for the setting up by HMRC-approved accounts managers of plans in the form of an account (an ISA) under which individuals may make certain investments, for the conditions under which they may invest and under which the accounts are to operate, for relief from tax in respect of account investments, and for general administration. The regulations generally took effect on 6 April 1999 and are summarised below.

General. An application to subscribe to an ISA may be made by an individual who is 18 or over (though see below as regards children under 18) and who is resident and ordinarily resident in the UK (or who is a non-UK resident Crown employee performing duties treated under *ICTA 1988, s 132(4)(a)* (see Tolley's Income Tax) as performed in the UK or, after 5 April 2001, who is married to, or a civil partner of, such an employee). Joint accounts are not permitted. An investor who subsequently fails to meet the residence requirement may retain the account and the right to tax exemptions thereunder but can make no further subscriptions to the account until he again comes to meet that requirement. After 7 January 2003, an application made on behalf of an individual suffering from mental disorder, by a parent, guardian, spouse, civil partner, son or daughter of his, is treated as if made by that individual. This replaced a rule specific to Scotland whereby a *curator bonis* appointed in respect of a qualifying individual incapable of managing his affairs could subscribe to an ISA in his capacity as such without affecting his right to subscribe in any other capacity.

An ISA is made up of *one or more* of the following: a stocks and shares component, a cash component and, for 2004/05 and earlier years, an insurance component. For details of investments qualifying for inclusion in each component, see Tolley's Income Tax. It must be designated from the outset as a maxi-account, mini-account or TESSA only account, such designation continuing to have effect for any year in which the investor makes a subscription to the account. The insurance component is abolished after 5 April 2005. After that date, life insurance products instead go into the stocks and shares component, except that certain low-risk products providing a 'cash-like' return go into the cash component. As regards insurance components in existence immediately before 6 April 2005, these are merged into either the stocks and shares component or the cash component, as appropriate. Where the insurance component was part of a maxi-account it is treated as merging on that date into the stocks and shares, or, as appropriate, cash component of that account. If the insurance component constituted a mini-account, it is treated as becoming on that date the stocks and shares, or, as appropriate, cash component of the same account.

A *maxi-account* must comprise a stocks and shares component (*with or without* other components). The maximum subscription per tax year (up to and including 2009/10) is £7,000 of which a maximum of £3,000 may be allocated to a cash component and, for 2004/05 and earlier years, £1,000 to an insurance component. In any tax year in which an investor subscribes to a maxi-account he cannot subscribe to any other ISA apart from a TESSA only account.

A *mini-account* must consist of a single specified component. The maximum subscription (per tax year) is £4,000 (£3,000 for 2004/05 and earlier years) if that component is stocks and shares, £3,000 if it is cash and, for 2004/05 and earlier years, £1,000 if it is insurance. In any tax year in which an investor subscribes to a mini-account, he cannot subscribe to another mini-account consisting of the same component or to a maxi-account.

A *TESSA only account* is an account consisting of a cash component only and limited to capital (*not* accumulated interest) transferred from a TESSA (see Tolley's Income Tax) within six months following its maturity after 5 April 1999 (or after 5 January 1999 where no follow-up TESSA is opened). Such transfers are not subject to any annual subscription limit, and may also be made to a maxi-account or to a cash component mini-account without counting towards the annual subscription limits for such accounts. Continuing subscriptions after 5 April 1999 to a TESSA or follow-up TESSA do not affect an individual's ISA annual subscription limits.

Subscriptions to an ISA must be made in cash (and must be allocated irrevocably to the agreed component or single component) except that

- shares acquired by the investor under a savings-related (SAYE) share option scheme (see **18.26** EMPLOYEE SHARE SCHEMES); or
- shares appropriated to him under an approved profit sharing scheme (see **18.29** EMPLOYEE SHARE SCHEMES); or
- plan shares (but not securities or other rights) of an approved share incentive plan (see **18.19** EMPLOYEE SHARE SCHEMES) which have ceased to be subject to the plan but remain in his beneficial ownership

may be transferred to a stocks and shares component. Such transfers count towards the annual subscription limits, by reference to the market value of the shares at the date of transfer. No chargeable gain or allowable loss arises on the transfer. A transfer of SAYE scheme shares must be made within 90 days after the exercise of the option. A transfer of shares appropriated under a profit sharing scheme must be made within 90 days after the earlier of the release date and the date on which the investor instructed the scheme trustees to transfer ownership of the shares to him. A transfer of share incentive plan shares must be made within 90 days after the shares ceased to be subject to the plan. In all cases, after 12 December 2000, 'shares' includes a reference to shares held in the form of depositary interests.

ISA investments cannot be purchased otherwise than out of cash held by the account manager and allocated to the particular component concerned, and cannot be purchased from the investor or his spouse or civil partner.

The title to ISA investments (other than cash deposits, national savings products and certain insurance policies) is vested in the account manager (or his nominee) either alone or jointly with the investor, though all ISA investments are in the beneficial ownership of the investor. The investor may elect to receive annual reports and accounts etc. in respect of ISA investments and/or to attend and vote at shareholders' etc. meetings.

The statements and declarations to be made when applying to subscribe to an ISA are specified. The maximum penalty for an incorrect statement or declaration is the amount (if any) of income tax and/or capital gains tax underpaid as a result. Assessments to withdraw tax relief or otherwise recover tax underpaid may be made on the account manager or investor. HMRC have power to require information from, and to inspect records of, account managers and investors.

From 1 October 2002 (and with reference to pre-existing ISAs as well as new ones), the terms and conditions of an ISA cannot prevent the investor from withdrawing funds or from transferring his account (or a part of it) to another HMRC-approved account manager (subject to the conditions governing such transfers). The account manager is allowed a reasonable business period (not exceeding 30 days) to comply with the investor's instructions in this regard. By concession, an ISA opened before 24 August 2002 offering a fixed or guaranteed return under terms requiring the funds to be locked in for a period of up to five years may, if the manager wishes and with Revenue agreement, continue to maturity under its original terms, though no further subscriptions can be made after 5 April 2003 (Revenue Press Release 26 July 2002).

Children under 18. For 2001/02 onwards, 16 and 17-year olds who otherwise satisfy the general conditions above may subscribe to a cash mini-account or to a cash component of a maxi-account. The maximum subscription for a tax year at the end of which the individual is under 18 is £3,000. The maximum ISA subscriptions for the tax year in which the individual reaches 18 are the same as for any other 18-year old, but no more than £3,000 can be subscribed before the individual's 18th birthday. See also under Tax Exemptions below.

Tax exemptions. Except as stated below, no income tax or capital gains tax is chargeable on the account manager or the investor in respect of interest, dividends, distributions, gains or (from 27 December 2005) alternative financial arrangement return on ISA investments. Capital losses are not allowable. As stated in the introduction above, tax credits on UK dividends paid before 6 April 2004 are repayable (via the account manager). An investor who ceases to be UK-resident is treated as continuing to be so resident as regards his entitlement to repayment of tax credits.'

The section headed 'Qualifying investments', running from the middle of page 335 to immediately before the heading 'Repairing invalid accounts' on page 339, is deleted.

References to *SI 2005 Nos 2561, 3230, 3350* are added to the list of statutory references on page 339.

20.46 **Friendly societies.** In the list of statutory references at the end, a reference to *SI 2005 No 2014* is added.

20.54 **Pension schemes.** The final paragraph is replaced by the following.

'*Pension Protection Fund.* The Treasury may make regulations providing for the application of certain taxes, including capital gains tax and corporation tax, in relation to the Board of the Pension Protection Fund and the funds that it controls. The current Regulations apply only for 2005/06 and provide that any gain accruing to the Board from disposals of investments are not chargeable gains if, or to the extent that, they were held for the purposes of the Pension Protection Fund or Fraud Compensation Fund. [*FA 2005, s 102; SI 2005 No 1907*].'

20.58   **Trade unions.** A reference to *SI 2005 No 3229, Reg 74* is added to the list of statutory instruments in the first paragraph.

20.77   The text is replaced by the following.

'**Married persons and civil partners.** Transfers between married persons and between civil partners are regarded as made on a no gain, no loss basis where the spouses or partners are living together. See **40.3** MARRIED PERSONS AND CIVIL PARTNERS.'

21   Fraudulent or Negligent Conduct

21.13   **HMRC practice in cases of serious tax fraud.** The text from the beginning up to (and including) the third paragraph from the end is replaced by the following.

'From 18 April 2005, criminal prosecutions for serious tax fraud in England and Wales are conducted by the Revenue and Customs Prosecutions Office, which is independent of HMRC. The Office has its own investigatory powers under *Serious Organised Crime and Police Act 2005, ss 60–62*. Before 18 April 2005, the Inland Revenue was itself a prosecuting authority and conducted its own prosecutions.

For new cases opened from 1 September 2005, the policy of the Commissioners of HMRC in cases of suspected serious tax fraud, as set out in Code of Practice COP 9 (2005), is as follows

1.   The Commissioners reserve complete discretion to pursue a criminal investigation with a view to prosecution where they consider it necessary and appropriate.

2.   Where a criminal investigation is not considered necessary or appropriate the Commissioners may decide to investigate using the civil investigation of fraud procedure.

3.   Where the Commissioners decide to investigate using the civil investigation of fraud procedure they will not seek a prosecution for the tax fraud which is the subject of that investigation. The taxpayer will be given an opportunity to make a full and complete disclosure of all irregularities in their tax affairs.

4.   However, where materially false statements are made or materially false documents are provided with intent to deceive, in the course of a civil investigation, the Commissioners may conduct a criminal investigation with a view to a prosecution of that conduct.

If the Commissioners decide to investigate using the civil investigation of fraud procedure the taxpayer will be given a copy of the above statement by an authorised officer.

Previously, the practice of the Board of Inland Revenue (and, after 18 April 2005, of HMRC) in cases of suspected serious tax fraud was set out in the so-called 'Hansard Statement' (last revised on 7 November 2002). This practice continues for investigations commenced before 1 September 2005. The practice was as follows.

(i)   The Board reserved complete discretion to pursue prosecutions in the circumstances they considered appropriate.

(ii)   Where serious tax fraud has been committed, they might accept a money settlement instead of pursuing a criminal prosecution.

(iii)   They would accept a money settlement, and would not pursue a criminal prosecution, if the taxpayer, in response to being given a copy of the Hansard Statement by an authorised officer (meaning a current serving member of Inland Revenue Special Compliance Office), made a full and complete confession of all tax irregularities.

(Revenue Internet Statement 8 November 2002; Revenue Tax Bulletin December 2002 pp 979–981). This replaced the previous Hansard Statement of 18 October 1990, which did not include the undertaking in (iii) above. Instead, the Board retained full discretion as to the course they would pursue. In considering this, it was the Board's practice to be *influenced* by the taxpayer's having made a full confession and given full co-operation during the investigation, but they gave no explicit assurance that they would not prosecute in such cases.

See also HMRC Code of Practice COP 9 (2005) and HMRC Internet Statement 20 December 2005.

A decision by HMRC to enter into a contract settlement (see **21.12** above) and not to prosecute does not preclude the Crown Prosecution Service (CPS) from instituting criminal proceedings (*R v W and another CA, [1998] STC 550*). However, the Revenue in commenting on this case stated that the CPS will ordinarily bring proceedings that encompass tax evasion charges only where that evasion is incidental to allegations of non-fiscal criminal conduct (Revenue Tax Bulletin June 1998 pp 544, 545).

HMRC's policy is to use the civil investigation of fraud procedure wherever possible. Criminal investigation is reserved for cases where HMRC needs to send a strong deterrent message or where the conduct involved is such that only a criminal sanction is appropriate. Circumstances in which HMRC will usually consider commencing a criminal, rather than civil, investigation include:

●   cases of organised or systematic fraud including conspiracy;

●   where an individual holds a position of trust or responsibility;

●   where materially false statements are made or materially false documents are provided in the course of a civil investigation;

●   where deliberate concealment, deception, conspiracy or corruption is suspected;

●   cases involving the use of false or forged documents;

●   cases involving money laundering;

●   where the perpetrator has committed previous offences or there is a repeated course of unlawful conduct or previous civil action;

●   cases involving theft, or the misuse or unlawful destruction of HMRC documents;

●   where there is evidence of assault on, threats to, or the impersonation of HMRC officials; and

●   where there is a link to suspected wider criminality, whether domestic or international, involving offences not under the administration of HMRC.

When considering whether a case should be investigated under the civil investigation of fraud procedure or will be the subject of a criminal investigation, one factor considered by HMRC is whether the taxpayer has made a complete and unprompted disclosure of the offences committed.

(HMRC Internet Statement 20 December 2005).

The Board of Inland Revenue sought to prosecute where a taxpayer, having had his attention formally drawn to the Hansard statement, was given an opportunity to disclose irregularities and made false denials of irregularities or incomplete or incorrect disclosures. The Board were also likely to prosecute where there was evidence of tax fraud involving accountants, lawyers and other tax advisers (whether the fraud was on their own account or in connection with a client), persons involved in the administration of taxation or occupying a prominent position in the field of law or government, or personnel in government departments who were administering tax, benefits or law enforcement (including Revenue personnel).

(Revenue Internet Statement 15 July 2004).'

24   Government Securities

24.2   **Exempt securities.** A reference to *SI 2006 No 184* is added in the statutory references list in the third paragraph.

26   HMRC: Confidentiality of Information

26.2   The following is added at the end.

'(*l*)   From 6 April 2005, the **Financial Reporting Review Panel** or other person authorised under *Companies Act 1985, s 245C* (or NI equivalent) to apply to the court for a declaration that the annual accounts of a company do not comply with the requirements of that Act (or NI equivalent). HMRC may disclose information to such persons for the purpose of facilitating the taking of steps by that person to discover whether there are grounds for such an application or a determination by that person as to whether or not to make such an application. [*Companies Act, 1985, s 245C; Companies (Audit, Investigations and Community Enterprise) Act 2004, s 11; SI 2005 No 699*]. HMRC and the Financial Reporting Review Panel have entered into a memorandum of understanding governing the disclosure of information under these provisions. HMRC will only disclose information relating to accounting periods ending after 6 April 2005. See HMRC Internet Statement, 28 June 2005 and 2005 STI 1197.

(*m*)   **Serious Organised Crime Agency.** From a date to be determined, HMRC may disclose information to the Serious Organised Crime Agency for the purpose of the exercise of the Agency's functions. [*Serious Organised Crime and Police Act 2005, s 34*].'

27   HMRC Explanatory Publications

27.1   **HMRC Explanatory Pamphlets.** The preamble to the list is replaced by the following.

'HMRC publish explanatory pamphlets (with supplements from time to time) on what were formerly Inland Revenue taxes. Those having a bearing on capital gains tax and corporation tax on chargeable gains are listed below, with the date of the latest edition in brackets, and are obtainable free of charge (except where otherwise stated) from local tax offices or from the internet (at www.hmrc.gov.uk). Alternatively, many can be ordered from the HMRC Orderline on 08459 000404 (or by fax on 08459 000604) or by post from PO Box 37, St. Austell, Cornwall PL25 5YN. HMRC have now withdrawn a substantial number of pamphlets and the information formerly contained in them is now available from their website.'

The following updated pamphlets are included in the list:

IR 65   Giving to Charity by Individuals (November 2005).

COP 9 (2005)   Civil investigation of fraud (November 2005).

The following pamphlets are removed from the list as withdrawn by HMRC.

IR 6   Double taxation relief for companies (March 1994).

IR 68   Accrued Income Scheme (December 2002).

IR 87   Letting and your home (December 1999).

IR 95   Approved profit sharing schemes: An outline for employees (June 1996).

IR 96   Approved profit sharing schemes: Explanatory notes (June 1996).

IR 97	Approved SAYE share option schemes: An outline for employees (June 1996)
IR 98	Approved SAYE share option schemes: Explanatory notes (August 2002).
IR 101	Approved company share option plans — An outline for employees (June 1996).
IR 102	Company share options: Explanatory notes (June 1996).
IR 131	Statements of Practice as at 31 August 2003 (available on the internet only) (March 2004).
IR 137	The Enterprise Investment Scheme (January 2003).
IR 152	Trusts – An Introduction (September 2004).
IR 166	The Euro — Tax Implications for UK Individuals and Businesses from 1 January 2002 (February 2002).
IR 167	Charter for Inland Revenue taxpayers (July 2003).
IR 169	Venture Capital Trusts — A Brief Guide (November 2002).
IR 2000	The Corporate Venturing Scheme (January 2001).
IR 2002	Share Incentive Plan — A Guide for Employees (October 2001).
IR 2005	Share Incentive Plans (guidance for employers and advisers) (October 2001).
IR 2006	Enterprise Management Incentives — A Guide (November 2001).
IR 2008	ISAs, PEPs and TESSAs (January 2005).
IR 2010	Paying Tax and NICs Electronically (February 2004).
IR 2013	Record-Keeping for Self-Assessment (January 2002).
—	A Guide to Corporation Tax Self-Assessment — for Tax Practitioners and Inland Revenue Officers, explaining the rules of CTSA. (Obtainable by post from Inland Revenue Library, Room 28, New Wing, Somerset House, Strand, London WC2R 1LB or in person from the Inland Revenue Information Centre as above — price £15.00 post-free.) (April 1999).
—	Guidance Notes for Charities (available on the internet at www.inlandrevenue.gov.uk/charities/index.htm) (November 2000).
—	Guidelines on the Tax Treatment of Appeal Funds (available on the internet at www.inlandrevenue.gov.uk/afg/afg.pdf) (May 2001).

27.3   **HMRC Tax Bulletin.** The telephone numbers are replaced by a single number 020–7147 2317.

27.4   **HMRC helpsheets.** The contact numbers are replaced by tel. 08459 000404, fax 08459 000604.

---

29   HMRC Statements of Practice

A note is added to SP 2/88 to indicate that the statement was withdrawn from February 2006.

One new statement is added to the list as follows.

'SP 1/06   **Self-assessment — finality and discovery.** HMRC set out their views on finality of self-assessments and discovery following the decision in *Veltema v Langham*. See **5.2** ASSESSMENTS.'

30   Hold-Over Reliefs

30.5 **Restrictions on, and clawback of, hold-over relief under TCGA 1992, s 165, Sch 7 as applicable to disposals after 13 March 1989.** The last sentence of the section headed 'Gifts to foreign-controlled companies' is replaced by the following.

'See *Foulser and another v MacDougall Ch D 2005, [2006] STC 311*, in which a complex avoidance scheme failed because of the application of this provision. The taxpayers' contention that the application of *section 167* to their case was incompatible with the EC Treaty was rejected by the Court.'

The last three sentences of the first paragraph of the section headed 'Emigration of transferee' are replaced by the following.

'For the latter purpose, a disposal does not include a no gain/no loss disposal between married persons or civil partners (see **40.3 MARRIED PERSONS AND CIVIL PARTNERS**) under *TCGA 1992, s 58*. If such a transfer occurs, a disposal by the acquiring spouse or civil partner is treated as made by the spouse or partner who originally acquired the asset to which the held-over gain related. If not paid within twelve months from the due date of payment, tax on the deemed gain assessed on the transferee can be assessed on the transferor within six years after the end of the year of assessment in which the disposal for which hold-over relief was claimed was made, although the transferor then has the right to recover any tax so paid from the transferee.'

In the list of statutory references near the end of that section, a reference to *SI 2005 No 3229, Reg 112* is added.

In the section headed 'Gifts to settlor-interested settlements', the third, fourth and fifth paragraphs on page 400 are replaced by the following.

'A settlor has an interest in a settlement if

(i)   any property which may at any time be comprised in the settlement or any 'derived property' is, or will or may become, payable to or applicable for the benefit of the settlor or his spouse or civil partner in any circumstances whatsoever, or

(ii)   the settlor, or his spouse or civil partner, enjoys a benefit deriving directly or indirectly from any property which is comprised in the settlement or any derived property.

References to the spouse or civil partner of the settlor in (i) and (ii) above do not include a spouse or civil partner from whom the settlor is separated under a court order, separation agreement or in circumstances such that the separation is likely to be permanent, or the widow, widower or surviving civil partner of the settlor.

A settlor does not have an interest under (i) above if and so long as none of the property which may at any time be comprised in the settlement and no derived property can become applicable or payable as mentioned in (i) above except in the event of:

● in the case of a marriage settlement or civil partnership settlement, the death of both the parties to the marriage or partnership and all or any of the children of one or both of the parities to the marriage or partnership (for disposals before 5 December 2005, all or any of the children of the marriage); or

● the death of a child of the settlor who had become beneficially entitled to the property or any derived property at an age not exceeding 25.'

The two paragraphs immediately preceding the final paragraph of the section are replaced by the following.

'An HMRC officer may require by notice a trustee, a beneficiary or a settlor (or the spouse or civil partner of a settlor or a person who has been the spouse or civil partner of a settlor at any time after the making of the relevant disposal) to give him such particulars as he thinks necessary for the purposes of the above provisions within such time as he may direct, not being less than 28 days.

[*TCGA 1992, ss 169B–169G; FA 2004, s 116, Sch 21 paras 4, 10(4); SI 2005 No 3229, Regs 113–115*].'

30.9   **General relief for gifts from 1980 to 1989.** In the list of statutory references immediately before the final paragraph, a reference to *SI 2005 No 3229, Reg 111* is added.

30.11   **Election to disapply incorporation relief.** The first paragraph is replaced by the following.

'On a transfer (of a business) that is within **30.10** above and takes place after 5 April 2002, the transferor may make an election to the effect that the incorporation relief under *TCGA 1992, s 162* should not apply. The election must be made by notice in writing to the Revenue. The deadline for making it is normally the second anniversary of 31 January following the tax year in which the transfer takes place. If, however, by the end of the tax year following that in which the transfer takes place, the transferor has disposed of *all* the 'new assets' (see below), the deadline is brought forward by one year. For this purpose, a transfer within *TCGA 1992, s 58* (see **40.3** MARRIED PERSONS AND CIVIL PARTNERS) is not counted as a disposal, but a subsequent disposal by the recipient spouse or civil partner (other than a transfer back to the original spouse or partner) counts as a disposal by the original spouse or partner.'

A reference to *SI 2005 No 3229, Reg 111* is added to the list of statutory references at the bottom of page 409.

31   Indexation

31.1   **Indexation allowance.** The updated RPI (Retail Prices Index) Table is as set out below.

	1982	1983	1984	1985	1986	1987	1988	1989	1990	1991
January	—	82.61	86.84	91.20	96.25	100.0	103.3	111.0	119.5	130.2
February	—	82.97	87.20	91.94	96.60	100.4	103.7	111.8	120.2	130.9
March	79.44	83.12	87.48	92.80	96.73	100.6	104.1	112.3	121.4	131.4
April	81.04	84.28	88.64	94.78	97.67	101.8	105.8	114.3	125.1	133.1
May	81.62	84.64	88.97	95.21	97.85	101.9	106.2	115.0	126.2	133.5
June	81.85	84.84	89.20	95.41	97.79	101.9	106.6	115.4	126.7	134.1
July	81.88	85.30	89.10	95.23	97.52	101.8	106.7	115.5	126.8	133.8
August	81.90	85.68	89.94	95.49	97.82	102.1	107.9	115.8	128.1	134.1
September	81.85	86.06	90.11	95.44	98.30	102.4	108.4	116.6	129.3	134.6
October	82.26	86.36	90.67	95.59	98.45	102.9	109.5	117.5	130.3	135.1
November	82.66	86.67	90.95	95.92	99.29	103.4	110.0	118.5	130.0	135.6
December	82.51	86.89	90.87	96.05	99.62	103.3	110.3	118.8	129.9	135.7

	1992	1993	1994	1995	1996	1997	1998	1999	2000	2001
January	135.6	137.9	141.3	146.0	150.2	154.4	159.5	163.4	166.6	171.1
February	136.3	138.8	142.1	146.9	150.9	155.0	160.3	163.7	167.5	172.0
March	136.7	139.3	142.5	147.5	151.5	155.4	160.8	164.1	168.4	172.2
April	138.8	140.6	144.2	149.0	152.6	156.3	162.6	165.2	170.1	173.1
May	139.3	141.1	144.7	149.6	152.9	156.9	163.5	165.6	170.7	174.2
June	139.3	141.0	144.7	149.8	153.0	157.5	163.4	165.6	171.1	174.4
July	138.8	140.7	144.0	149.1	152.4	157.5	163.0	165.1	170.5	173.3
August	138.9	141.3	144.7	149.9	153.1	158.5	163.7	165.5	170.5	174.0
September	139.4	141.9	145.0	150.6	153.8	159.3	164.4	166.2	171.7	174.6
October	139.9	141.8	145.2	149.8	153.8	159.5	164.5	166.5	171.6	174.3
November	139.7	141.6	145.3	149.8	153.9	159.6	164.4	166.7	172.1	173.6
December	139.2	141.9	146.0	150.7	154.4	160.0	164.4	167.3	172.2	173.4

	2002	2003	2004	2005	2006
January	173.3	178.4	183.1	188.9	193.4
February	173.8	179.3	183.8	189.6	194.2
March	174.5	179.9	184.6	190.5	
April	175.7	181.2	185.7	191.6	
May	176.2	181.5	186.5	192.0	
June	176.2	181.3	186.8	192.2	
July	175.9	181.3	186.8	192.2	
August	176.4	181.6	187.4	192.6	
September	177.7	182.5	188.1	193.1	
October	177.9	182.6	188.6	193.3	
November	178.2	182.7	189.0	193.6	
December	178.5	183.5	189.9	194.1	

---

33   Interest on Overpaid Tax

33.1   **Persons other than companies — 1996/97 onwards (self-assessment).** Recent interest rates are as follows.

2.25% p.a. from 6 September 2005

3.00% p.a. from 6 September 2004 to 5 September 2005

2.25% p.a. from 6 December 2003 to 5 September 2004

1.50% p.a. from 6 August 2003 to 5 December 2003

2.25% p.a. from 6 November 2001 to 5 August 2003

3.00% p.a. from 6 May 2001 to 5 November 2001

The following is added immediately after the list.

'HMRC announced on 6 September 2005 that the interest rates that they had previously used for the period 6 May 2001 to 5 September 2005 were incorrect. The above rates are the corrected rates published on 6 September 2005. The incorrect rates used were higher than those above but HMRC will not make any attempt to recover any amounts overpaid. Where, however, a repayment is reviewed for other reasons, the correct amount of interest will be calculated. (HMRC News Release 6 September 2005).'

33.2   **Persons other than companies — 1995/96 and earlier years.** Recent interest rates are as in 33.1 above.

33.3   **Companies.** Recent interest rates for accounting periods ending **on or after 1 July 1999** for amounts overpaid **on or after the normal due date** are as follows.

3.00% p.a. from 6 September 2005

4.00% p.a. from 6 September 2004 to 5 September 2005

3.00% p.a. from 6 December 2003 to 5 September 2004

Recent interest rates for accounting periods ending **on or after 1 July 1999** for amounts overpaid **before the normal due date**, for example under the quarterly accounting rules for large companies, are as follows.

4.25% p.a. from 15 August 2005

4.50% p.a. from 16 August 2004 to 14 August 2005

4.25% p.a. from 21 June 2004 to 15 August 2004

4.00% p.a. from 17 May 2004 to 20 June 2004

These rates apply up to the earlier of the date of repayment and the normal due date (after which the normal rates apply).

Recent interest rates for accounting periods ending **before 1 July 1999** are as follows.

2.00% p.a. from 6 September 2005

2.75% p.a. from 6 September 2004 to 5 September 2005

2.00% p.a. from 6 December 2003 to 5 September 2004

Recent interest rates for accounting periods ending **before 1 October 1993** are as follows.

5.00% p.a. from 6 September 2005

5.75% p.a. from 6 September 2004 to 5 September 2005

5.00% p.a. from 6 December 2003 to 5 September 2004

---

34   Interest and Surcharges on Unpaid Tax

34.1   **Persons other than companies —1996/97 onwards (self-assessment) and assessments raised after 5 April 1998.** Recent interest rates are as follows.

6.50% p.a. from 6 September 2005

7.50% p.a. from 6 September 2004 to 5 September 2005

6.50% p.a. from 6 December 2003 to 5 September 2004

34.2   **Persons other than companies — assessments for 1995/96 and earlier years raised before 6 April 1998.** Recent interest rates are as in **34.1** above.

34.6   **Companies.** Recent interest rates for accounting periods ending **on or after 1 July 1999** for tax becoming due **on or after the normal due date** are as follows.

6.50% p.a. from 6 September 2005

7.50% p.a. from 6 September 2004 to 5 September 2005

6.50% p.a. from 6 December 2003 to 5 September 2004

Recent interest rates for accounting periods ending **on or after 1 July 1999** for tax payable **before the normal due date** under the quarterly accounting rules for large companies are as follows.

5.5% p.a. from 15 August 2005

5.75% p.a. from 16 August 2004 to 14 August 2005

5.50% p.a. from 21 June 2004 to 15 August 2004

5.25% p.a. from 17 May 2004 to 20 June 2004

These rates apply up to the earlier of the date of payment and the normal due date (after which the normal rates apply).

Recent interest rates for accounting periods ending **before 1 July 1999** are as follows.

5.25% p.a. from 6 September 2005

6.00% p.a. from 6 September 2004 to 5 September 2005

5.25% p.a. from 6 December 2003 to 5 September 2004

The following is added immediately after the list of rates.

'HMRC announced on 6 September 2005 that the interest rate that they had previously used for the period 6 December 2003 to 5 September 2004 was incorrect. The rate for that period shown above is the corrected rate published on 6 September 2005. The incorrect rate used was lower than that above but HMRC will not make any attempt to recover any further interest due. Where, however, a liability is reviewed for other reasons, the correct amount of interest will be calculated. (HMRC News Release 6 September 2005).'

Recent interest rates for accounting periods ending **before 1 October 1993** are as follows.

5.00% p.a. from 6 September 2005

5.75% p.a. from 6 September 2004 to 5 September 2005

5.00% p.a. from 6 December 2003 to 5 September 2004

35   Land

35.8   **Small part disposals.** The third paragraph and (*a*) and (*b*) are replaced by the following.

'The provisions do not apply to

(*a*)   transfers treated as giving rise to neither a gain nor a loss between spouses or civil partners (see **40.3** MARRIED PERSONS AND CIVIL PARTNERS) or between companies in the same group (see **12.11** COMPANIES); or (*b*)   an estate or interest in land which is a wasting asset (e.g. a short lease under **35.14** below).'

36   Life Insurance Policies and Deferred Annuities

36.1   **Introduction.** The third paragraph is replaced by the following.

'For the above purposes, '*actual consideration*' is consideration other than consideration deemed to be given under any provision relating to tax on chargeable gains. Amounts paid under the policy or contract by way of premiums or as lump sum consideration are not actual consideration. Actual consideration given for a disposal made by one spouse or civil partner to the other, an 'approved post-marriage disposal', an 'approved post-civil partnership disposal', or an intra-group transfer to which *TCGA 1992, s 171(1)* (see **12.12** COMPANIES) applies, is treated as not being actual consideration. A disposal is an '*approved post-marriage disposal*' or an '*approved post-civil partnership disposal*' if it is one made in consequence of the dissolution or annulment of a marriage or civil partnership by one party to the marriage or partnership to the other, with the approval, agreement or authority of, or pursuant to an order of, a court (or other person or body) having jurisdiction under the law of any country or territory, where the rights or interest disposed of were held by the person making the disposal immediately before the marriage or partnership was dissolved or annulled. An '*interest*' in relation to any rights is an interest as co-owner of the rights, whether the rights are owned jointly or in common and whether or not the interests of the co-owners are equal.'

A reference to *SI 2005 No 3229, Reg 116* is added to the list of references near the foot of page 468.

36.2   **Income tax.** A reference to *SI 2005 No 3229, Reg 76* is added to the list of references at the end.

37   Loan Relationships of Companies

37.5   **Computation.** The second and third paragraphs on page 474 are replaced by the following.

'Subject to specified exceptions, amounts recognised for accounting purposes in a company's statement of recognised gains and losses or statement of changes in equity for the first accounting period of the company beginning on or after 1 January 2005 which represent a prior period adjustment are not brought into account in that accounting period but are instead to be brought into account over a period of ten years beginning with first accounting period of the company beginning on or after 1 January 2006. There are anti-avoidance provisions to prevent companies avoiding the deferment of a debit under these provisions.

[*FA 1996, ss 85A, 85B, 103(1); FA 2004, s 52, Sch 10 paras 3, 17; FA 2005, s 82, Sch 4 paras 26, 50; SI 2004 No 3271; SI 2005 No 3383*].'

In the middle of the paragraph headed 'Foreign exchange gains and losses', references to *SI 2005 No 2012, Regs 4, 6; SI 2005 No 3374, Regs 3, 4, 6* and *SI 2005 No 3422* are added to the list of references. The final sentence of the paragraph is amended to read as follows.

'Matched differences are normally brought into account, as chargeable gains or allowable capital losses as appropriate, when the matched asset is disposed of (see *SI 2002 No 1970* as amended by *SI 2004 No 3259; SI 2005 No 2013*).'

37.17   **Transitional rules affecting individuals.** The text of section (a) is replaced by the following.

'No chargeable gain will arise where a 'relevant person' holds a qualifying indexed security at 5 April 1996 for which there is no disposal neither actual nor deemed. However, if at any time after 5 April 1996 a relevant event occurs the chargeable gain will be calculated as if the disposal had occurred at 5 April 1996 and the consideration was equal to the market value at 5 April 1996. This does not apply to disposals between spouses or civil partners under *TCGA 1992, s 58* (see **40.3** MARRIED PERSONS AND CIVIL PARTNERS) but will apply to a subsequent disposal by the other spouse.

[*FA 1996, s 105, Sch 15 para 27; SI 2005 No 3229, Reg 130*].'

38   Losses

38.9   **Assets of negligible value.** The last two paragraphs are replaced by the following.

'For HMRC practice and procedure, see HMRC Capital Gains Manual CG 13128–13133. HMRC have extended their post-transaction valuation checking service (see **53.4** RETURNS) to negligible value claims. Form CG34 must be submitted at the same time or after the claim is made. Acceptance by HMRC of the value submitted does not mean that they necessarily accept that all the conditions for the claim are met or that any allowable loss arises. (HMRC Internet Statement 31 January 2006).

Quoted securities. HMRC have accepted that certain quoted securities have become of negligible value within the meaning of *TCGA 1992, s 24(2)*. For securities so accepted in recent years (up to 28 February 2006), see the HMRC website (at www.hmrc.gov.uk).'

38.10   **Loans to traders.** In the second line, the words 'or civil partners' are inserted immediately after 'spouses'.

The list of statutory references towards the end of the first paragraph is replaced by the following.

'[*TCGA 1992, s 253(3)(12)(14)(a)(aa), (15); FA 1996, Sch 14 para 65, Sch 15 para 7(a), Sch 39 para 8; SI 2005 No 3229, Reg 120*].'

A reference to *SI 2005 No 3229, Reg 120* is added to the list of statutory references at the end of the first paragraph of the section headed 'Relief for payment made under guarantee'.

38.13   **Losses on shares in unlisted trading companies: individuals.** The penultimate paragraph on page 499 is replaced by the following.

'An individual '*subscribes*' for shares if they are issued to him by the company for money or money's worth, or if they were so issued to his 'spouse' or 'civil partner', who transferred them to him by a transaction inter vivos. '*Spouse*' refers to one of two spouses who are living together and '*civil partner*' refers to one of two civil partners who are living together (see **40.2** MARRIED PERSONS AND CIVIL PARTNERS).'

Immediately before the section headed 'Application to EIS shares', a reference to *SI 2005 No 3229, Regs 77, 78* is added to the list of statutory references.

39   Market Value

39.4   **Unquoted shares.** A reference to *Shinebond Ltd v Carrol (Sp C 522), 2006 STI 591* is added at the end of the penultimate paragraph.

40   Married Persons and Civil Partners

40.1A   The following new section is added.

'**Civil partners.** *FA 2005* includes provisions enabling the Treasury to make regulations providing for same-sex partners in a 'civil partnership' to be treated for tax purposes in the same way as married persons. For this purpose a '*civil partnership*' is one which exists under or by virtue of the *Civil Partnerships Act 2004* and '*civil partner*' is to be construed accordingly. [*FA 2005, s 103*]. The regulations, the *Tax and Civil Partnership Regulations 2005 SI 2005 No 3229*, take effect from 5 December 2005, the date from which the *Civil Partnership Act 2004* comes into effect.

Transfers of assets between civil partners who are living together are treated as made on a 'no gain/no loss basis' as in **40.3** below.

Civil partners living together may claim exemption in respect of only one main residence. See **47.1** PRIVATE RESIDENCES.'

40.2   '**Living together'.** The text is replaced by the following.

'Individuals who are married to, or are civil partners of, each other are treated as living together unless they are

(*a*)   separated under a court order or separation deed, or

(*b*)   in fact separated in circumstances which render permanent separation likely.

[*ICTA 1988, s 282; TCGA 1992, s 288(3); SI 2005 No 3229, Regs 62, 122*].

Both (*a*) and (*b*) above require the marriage or civil partnership to have broken down (HMRC Capital Gains Manual CG 22074). As regards (*b*), HMRC give further guidance in their Relief Manual at RE 1060–1065.'

40.3   **Transfers between spouses or civil partners.** The first four paragraphs are replaced by the following.

'Transfers of assets, in a year of assessment, between spouses or civil partners who are living together (see **40.2** above) in any part of that year are regarded as made on a 'no gain/no loss' basis. This treatment also applies to transfers between spouses or civil partners in the part of a year following the start of the marriage or civil partnership and in the whole of the year in which separation takes place, even though the spouses or civil partners may not be 'living together' at the time of transfer (but does not apply following a decree absolute). The no gain/ no loss treatment does not apply to transfers (i) by way of *donatio mortis causa* (see **15.4** DEATH); or (ii) to or from trading stock of either spouse or civil partner. [*TCGA 1992, s 58; SI 2005 No 3229, Reg 107*].

The deemed consideration for a no gain/no loss transfer between spouses or civil partners is thus equal to the transferor's acquisition cost for CGT purposes, including any enhancement expenditure, plus indexation allowance to date or to April 1998 if earlier (see **31** INDEXATION). The no gain/no loss rule cannot be disapplied, and any *actual* consideration given for the transfer is ignored. It should be noted that the transaction is still a disposal by the transferor spouse or partner and an acquisition by the transferee as at the date of transfer; the legislation does not operate by deeming no disposal to have taken place (though see **60.14** TAPER RELIEF which combines the periods for which the asset is held by each spouse or partner but which applies only for the purpose of computing that relief).

Where either spouse or civil partner is non-UK resident, but the definition at **40.2** above nevertheless treats them as 'living together', there is no authority for disapplying the no gain/ no loss treatment even if the transfer results in an asset leaving the UK tax net (see Revenue

Capital Gains Manual CG 22304 and see *Gubay v Kington HL 1984, 57 TC 601*).

See **16.6** DISPOSAL for part disposals between spouses or civil partners and **35.8** LAND for small part disposals of land.'

The text after the example is replaced by the following.

'A **transfer of shares or securities** between spouses or civil partners under the no gain/no loss rule can cause conflict between the rules at **58.2** SHARES AND SECURITIES — IDENTIFICATION RULES which treat the shares as acquired by the transferee at the date of transfer and those at **60.14** TAPER RELIEF which treat them for taper relief purposes as acquired by the transferee at the time they were acquired by the transferor. In practice, this is a problem only if the transferor acquired the shares at different times *and* the transferee's disposal is a part disposal. An article in Revenue Tax Bulletin August 2001 pp 876, 877, with worked example, explains HMRC's pragmatic approach, and is also a useful illustration of how the no gain/no loss rule, the share identification rules and the taper relief rules generally interact.

Transfers whilst spouses separated or treated as separated. In a case in which spouses, after several years of separation, were divorced and the court order (by consent) on the decree nisi provided for the transfer of certain property (which was not otherwise exempt) it was held that the property had been disposed of at the time of the decree nisi. As the divorce was not then absolute, the spouses were still connected persons and the consideration was to be taken as the market value. See **13.1** CONNECTED PERSONS and **39.1** MARKET VALUE and HMRC Capital Gains Manual CG 22400–22510. The normal 'no gain/no loss' basis did not apply as the spouses were not living together. (*Aspden v Hildesley Ch D 1981, 55 TC 609*).

Unmarried couples. The no gain/no loss rule applies only to transfers between persons legally recognised as married or as civil partners under English or Scottish law. Polygamous marriages may be so recognised in limited circumstances (see HMRC Capital Gains Manual CG 22072). The rule does not apply to a transfer to a so-called 'common-law' husband or wife. An unmarried couple or a couple who are not civil partners are not CONNECTED PERSONS (**13**) by reason of their relationship alone (though they may be for other reasons, for example if they are also business partners). However, a transfer of an asset between them is likely to be treated as taking place at MARKET VALUE (see **39.1**) unless made at arm's length in any case.'

40.4   **Civil partnerships.** This section is deleted (and replaced by the new text at **40.1A**).

---

42   Offshore Settlements

42.6   **Test whether settlor has an interest.** All of the text after list (*a*) to (*c*) is replaced by the following.

'Each of the following is a '*defined person*':

● the settlor;

● the settlor's spouse;

● the settlor's civil partner;

● any child (which term includes stepchild) of the settlor or of the settlor's spouse or civil partner;

● the spouse or civil partner of any such child;

● any grandchild of the settlor or of the settlor's spouse or civil partner (see **42.7** below as regards the addition of grandchildren to the list of defined persons); ('*grandchild*' includes a child of a stepchild or a stepchild of a child or stepchild);

- the spouse or civil partner of any such grandchild (see **42.7** below as regards the addition of grandchildren and their spouses or civil partners to the list of defined persons);

- a company controlled by a person or persons mentioned in the foregoing (see **42.7** below as regards the addition of grandchildren and their spouses or civil partners to the fore-mentioned categories); ('*control*' is construed as in *ICTA 1988, s 416* but for these purposes no rights or powers of (or attributed to) an associate or associates of a person are attributed to him under *ICTA 1988, s 416(6)* if he is not a participator (within *ICTA 1988, s 417(1)*, but subject to ESC D40 (see **42.9** below)) in the company);

- a company associated with any such company; ('*associated*' is construed as in *ICTA 1988, s 416* but for these purposes where it falls to be decided whether a company is controlled by a person or persons, a similar relaxation to that for '*control*' applies as above).

A settlor does not have an interest in a settlement at any time when none of the property or income concerned can become applicable or payable as mentioned above except in the event of:

- the bankruptcy of some person who is or may become beneficially entitled to that property or income;

- any assignment of or charge on the property or income being made or given by some such person;

- in the case of a marriage settlement or civil partnership settlement, the death of both parties to the marriage or civil partnership and of all or any of the children of one or both of the parties to the marriage or civil partnership (before 5 December, all or any of the children of the marriage); or

- the death under the age of 25 or some lower age of some person who would be beneficially entitled to the property or income on attaining that age.

He also does not have an interest in a settlement under (*a*) above at any time when some person is alive and under the age of 25 if during that person's life none of the property or income concerned can become applicable or payable as mentioned in (*a*) above except in the event of that person becoming bankrupt or assigning or charging his interest in the property or income concerned.

[*TCGA 1992, Sch 5 para 2; FA 1998, s 131, Sch 22 para 2; SI 2005 No 3229, Reg 126(2)*].'

42.7   **Addition of grandchildren to list of defined persons**. The words 'or civil partner' are added after 'spouse' in the first line.

The last two paragraphs are replaced by the following.

'The persons mentioned in (*c*) and (*d*) above are: any grandchild (as in **42.6** above) of the settlor or of the settlor's spouse or civil partner, the spouse or civil partner of any such grandchild, a company controlled by any such grandchildren and/or their spouses or civil partners (with or without other defined persons — see **42.6** above) and a company associated with any such company. (For these purposes, '*control*' and '*associated*' are to be construed as in **42.6** above.)

[*TCGA 1992, Sch 5 para 2A; FA 1998, Sch 22 para 2; SI 2005 No 3229, Reg 126(3)*].'

42.8   **Exceptions to charge.** The remaining text after the first paragraph is replaced by the following.

'There is also no charge on the settlor where **both** (*a*) and (*b*) below apply.

(*a*)   The settlor has no interest in the settlement at any time in the year except for one (or, where they are satisfied by reference to the same person, for two or all) of the following reasons:

● property is, or will or may become, applicable for the benefit of or payable to a person, being the settlor's spouse or civil partner, any child (which term includes stepchild) or grandchild (defined as in **42.6** above, and see below for the addition of grandchildren to this list) of the settlor or of the settlor's spouse or civil partner, or the spouse or civil partner of any such child or grandchild;

● income is, or will or may become applicable for the benefit of or payable to such a person; or

● such a person enjoys a benefit from property or income.

(*b*)   Either

● the person referred to in (*a*) above dies in the year; or

● where the person referred to in (*a*) above is the settlor's spouse or civil partner or the spouse or civil partner of any child or grandchild of the settlor or of the settlor's spouse or civil partner, that person ceases to be married to, or to be a civil partner of, the settlor, the child or the grandchild concerned (as the case may be) during the year.

Again no charge arises on the settlor in the following circumstances:

(i)   the settlor has no interest in the settlement at any time in the year except for the reason that there are two or more persons, each of whom is one of the following: the settlor's spouse or civil partner, any child (which term includes stepchild) or grandchild (defined as in **42.6** above, and see below for the addition of grandchildren to this list) of the settlor or of the settlor's spouse or civil partner, or the spouse or civil partner of any such child or grandchild and stands to gain for one or more of the following reasons:

● property is, or will or may become, applicable for his benefit or payable to him;

● the income is, or will or may become, applicable for his benefit or payable to him; or

● he enjoys a benefit from property or income, *and*

(ii)   each of the persons referred to in (i) dies in the year.

References above to grandchildren apply only in relation to disposals made **on or after 17 March 1998** to which the 'charge on settlor' provisions would otherwise apply by reference to grandchildren (see **42.6** and **42.7** above).

[*TCGA 1992, Sch 5 paras 3–5; FA 1998, Sch 22 para 3; SI 2005 No 3229, Reg 126(4)*].'

42.10   **Qualifying settlements, and commencement.** The third paragraph is replaced by the following.

'A settlement is a '*protected settlement*' at any time if at that time the 'beneficiaries' are confined to persons falling within some or all of the following categories:

● children of a settlor or of a spouse or civil partner of a settlor who are under 18 either at that time or at the end of the immediately preceding tax year;

● unborn children of a settlor, of a spouse or civil partner of a settlor, or of a future spouse or civil partner of a settlor;

● future spouses or civil partners of any children or future children of a settlor, a spouse or civil partner of a settlor or any future spouse or civil partner of a settlor;

● a future spouse or civil partner of a settlor;

• persons who are not at that time defined persons (see **42.6** above) in relation to the settlement and by reference to any current settlor.

Despite the addition of grandchildren to the list of defined persons (see **42.7** above), HMRC do *not* regard the existence as beneficiaries of the settlor's (or his spouse's) grandchildren (of whatever age) as denying protected settlement status (Revenue Tax Bulletin December 1998 p 620).'

A reference to *SI 2005 No 3229, Reg 126(5)* is added to the list of statutory references in the penultimate paragraph.

---

46 Penalties

46.26 **Liability under criminal law.** The Revenue's Statement of Practice 2/88, described here, has now been withdrawn. For HMRC's practice in considering whether to accept a money settlement or institute criminal proceedings for fraud, see now **21.13** FRAUDULENT OR NEGLIGENT CONDUCT.

---

47 Private Residences

47.1 **Exemption generally.** The eighth paragraph is replaced by the following.

'There can only be one main residence in the case of an individual and his spouse or civil partner living with him, so long as they are 'living together' (see **40.2** MARRIED PERSONS AND CIVIL PARTNERS). [*TCGA 1992, s 222(6); SI 2005 No 3229, Reg 117(2)*]. As regards separation or divorce, see **47.2**(*c*) below.'

The third complete paragraph on page 616 is replaced by the following.

'Where the individual has had different interests at different times, the period of ownership is taken for the purposes of *TCGA 1992, ss 222–226* generally (i.e. all the provisions contained in this chapter) to begin from the first acquisition taken into account in arriving at the amount of the allowable expenditure deductible in the computation of the gain to which *TCGA 1992, s 222(1)* above applies. In the case of an individual living with his spouse or civil partner

(A) if one disposes of, or of his interest in, the dwelling-house (or part) which is their only or main residence to the other, and in particular if it passes on death to the other as legatee, the other's period of ownership is treated as beginning with the beginning of the period of ownership of the one making the disposal, and

(B) if (A) above applies, but the dwelling-house (or part) was not the only or main residence of both throughout the period of ownership of the one making the disposal, account is taken of any part of that period during which it was his only or main residence as if it was also that of the other.

[*TCGA 1992, s 222(7); SI 2005 NO 3229, Reg 117(3)*].'

47.2 **Periods of ownership qualifying for exemption.** Section (*d*) is replaced by the following.

'**'Job-related' accommodation.** If at any time during an individual's period of ownership (as for *TCGA 1992, s 222(1)* in **47.1** above so that a period before 31 March 1982 is *not* ignored) of part or the whole of a dwelling-house he resides in 'job-related' living accommodation and he intends in due course to occupy the dwelling-house (or part) as his only or main residence, he is deemed at that time to occupy the dwelling-house (or part) as a residence for the purposes of *TCGA 1992, ss 222–226* (i.e. all the provisions contained in this chapter). Living accommodation is 'job-related' for these purposes if it is provided for a taxpayer by reason of his (or for his spouse or civil partner by reason of their) employment, in any of the following cases.

(i)   Where it is necessary for the proper performance of the duties of the employment that the employee should reside in that accommodation.

(ii)   Where the provision of such accommodation is customary and it is provided for the better performance of the duties of employment.

(iii)   Where there is a special threat to the employee's security, special security arrangements are in force, and the employee resides in the accommodation as part of those arrangements.

With certain exceptions, (i) and (ii) above do not apply to accommodation provided to its directors by a company (or associated company).

In respect of residence after 5 April 1983, living accommodation is also job-related if either the person claiming the relief or his or her spouse or civil partner is carrying on a trade, profession or vocation on premises or other land provided by another person, under tenancy or otherwise, and is bound under an arm's length contract to live in those premises or on other premises provided. Relief is not given if the accommodation is provided, in whole or in part, by a company in which the borrower, or his or her spouse or civil partner, has a material interest (as defined) or by any person or persons with whom he or she carries on a business in partnership. [*TCGA 1992, s 222(8)(8A)–(8D)(9); ICTA 1988, s 356; FA 1999, Sch 4 paras 17, 18(4); ITEPA 2003, Sch 6 para 213; SI 2005 No 3229, Reg 117(4)(5)]*.'

---

48   Qualifying Corporate Bonds

48.2   **Definition of corporate bond.** At (*a*) the case reference is updated to read '*Weston v Garnett CA, [2005] STC 1134*'.

---

51   Residence and Domicile

51.3   **Residence.** The second paragraph at (*a*) is amended to read as follows.

'The six months' rule is rigidly applied, even in cases of force majeure, and in border-line cases hours may be significant. See *Wilkie v CIR Ch D 1951, 32 TC 495* where 'six months' was held to mean six calendar months. Otherwise, to be regarded by HMRC as UK resident for a year of assessment an individual would normally have to be physically present in the UK at some time in the tax year and would also depend on the circumstances. See, for example, *Shepherd v HMRC (Sp C 484). [2005] SSCD 644*, in which an airline pilot who was in the UK for only 80 days in a tax year was nevertheless held to be resident in the UK for that year. HMRC treat, *with no exceptions* (including years after 1992/93), an individual as resident if he is in the UK for six months or more during the year. Six months are regarded as 183 days and days of arrival and departure are normally ignored (HMRC Pamphlet IR 20, December 1999 edition, para 1.2).'

51.5   **Visits abroad and claims to non-UK residence and to non-UK ordinary residence.** The following is added to the last paragraph.

'See *Shepherd v HMRC (Sp C 484). [2005] SSCD 644*, in which an airline pilot was held to have remained resident in the UK for a tax year in which he had been physically in the UK for only 80 days.'

51.6   **Companies.** The second case reference in the paragraph immediately following the bullet points is updated to read '*Wood and another v Holden CA, [2006] STC 443*'.

53   Returns

53.2   **Annual tax returns.** A reference to *SI 2005 No 3229, Reg 106* is added in the first list of statutory references in the second paragraph.

53.4   **Post-transaction valuation checks and rulings.** The following is added to the end of the first paragraph.

'From 31 January 2006, the service is extended to valuations of assets that are the subject of a negligible value claim (see **38.9** LOSSES).'

53.10   **Power to call for documents.** The following is added immediately before the final paragraph.

'The fact that a taxpayer has already supplied documents to HMRC in the course of a working families tax credit enquiry does not prevent HMRC from including those documents in a notice under *TMA 1970, s 19A* (*Low v HMRC Sp C 2005 (Sp C 510), [2006] SSCD 21*).'

53.25   **Issuing houses, stockbrokers, auctioneers, nominee shareholders etc.** The following is added at the end of the first paragraph.

'HMRC have published spreadsheet templates for making returns under this provision on their web site (www.hmrc.gov.uk).'

53.26   **Electronic lodgement of returns.** The first paragraph is replaced by the following.

'Subject to the conditions detailed below, returns under *TMA 1970, ss 8, 8A* and *12AA* (see **53.2, 53.18** above) may be lodged using HMRC's electronic lodgement service at any time before 31 March 2006. Any supporting documentation (including accounts, statements or reports) required to be delivered with a return may similarly be lodged electronically if the return is so lodged (or may instead be delivered by the last day for submission of the return).'

54   Rollover Relief — Replacement of Business Assets

54.3   **Qualifying assets.** Item 4 is amended to read as follows.

'Goodwill. See HMRC Capital Gains Manual CG 68000–68976 for consideration of what constitutes goodwill. See also *Balloon Promotions Ltd v Wilson, Sp C March 2006 (Sp C 524)* (in which the Special Commissioner criticised some aspects of HMRC's manual) and *Kirby v Thorn EMI plc CA 1987, 60 TC 519*.'

56   Settlements

56.3   **Liability of trustees, settlors and beneficiaries.** The final paragraph is replaced by the following.

'The Government is in the process of reforming the tax regime for trusts. A discussion paper specifically examining capital gains tax reform was published on the Revenue's website on 17 December 2003. A further consultation document was published on the website on 13 August 2004. Draft legislation was published on 2 February 2006.'

56.4   **Charge on settlors with interests in settlements.** The paragraphs following the list (*a*) to (*f*) are amended to read as follows.

'A settlor has an interest in a settlement if

(i)   any property which may at any time be comprised in the settlement or any derived property is, or will or may become, payable to or applicable for the benefit of the settlor or his spouse or civil partner in any circumstances whatsoever, or

(ii)   the settlor, or his spouse or civil partner, enjoys a benefit deriving directly or indirectly from any property which is comprised in the settlement or any derived property.

For 1995/96 onwards, references to the spouse or civil partner of the settlor in (i) and (ii) above do not include a person to whom the settlor is not for the time being married but may marry later, a person of whom the settlor is not for the time being a civil partner but of whom he may later be a civil partner, or a spouse or civil partner from whom the settlor is separated under a court order or similar arrangement that is likely to be permanent, or the widow, widower or surviving civil partner of the settlor.

A settlor does not have an interest under (i) above if and so long as

(A)   none of the property which may at any time be comprised in the settlement and no derived property can become applicable or payable as mentioned in (i) above except in the event of:

- the bankruptcy of some person who is or may become beneficially entitled to that property or any derived property;

- any assignment of or charge on that property or any derived property being made or given by some such person;

- in the case of a marriage settlement or civil partnership settlement, the death of both the parties to the marriage or civil partnership and all or any of the children of one or both of the parties to the marriage or civil partnership (before 5 December 2005, all or any of the children of the marriage); or

- the death of a child of the settlor who had become beneficially entitled to the property or any derived property at an age not exceeding 25; or

(B)   some person is alive and under the age of 25 during whose life the property or any derived property cannot become applicable or payable as mentioned in (i) above except in the event of that person becoming bankrupt or assigning or charging his interest in that property.

The settlor is excepted from the charge where

(I)   he has an interest in a settlement under (i) or (ii) above only because that property is, or will or may become, payable to or applicable for the benefit of his spouse or civil partner *or* his spouse or civil partner enjoys a benefit from property, or for both such reasons, and

(II)   his spouse or civil partner dies, or he and his spouse or civil partner cease to be married or to be civil partners of each other, during the year.'

56.16   **Anti-avoidance: deemed disposal of underlying assets on certain disposals of interests in settled property.** The two paragraphs immediately preceding the heading 'Prevention of double charge' are amended to read as follows.

'Where the settlor dies or the exception from the charge on settlor in **56.4** above on death of spouse or civil partner or end of marriage or civil partnership would apply, the above condition is treated as not present in the tax year of death or end of marriage or civil partnership.

[*TCGA 1992, Sch 4A para 4(2), paras 5–7, 12; SI 2005 No 3229, Reg 125*].'

57   Shares and Securities

57.18   **Personal equity plans.** In the list of statutory references at the end, references to *SI 2005 Nos 2562, 3348* are added.

60   Taper Relief

60.14   **Assets transferred between spouses or civil partners.** The text is amended to read as follows.

'On a disposal of an asset acquired from a spouse or civil partner under the no gain/no loss rule in *TCGA 1992, s 58* (see **40.3** MARRIED PERSONS AND CIVIL PARTNERS), taper relief applies as if the time when the transferee spouse or partner acquired the asset was the time when the transferor acquired it (or is treated as having acquired it, for example where there has been more than one inter-spouse or inter-partner transfer of the same asset). In other words, the combined period of holding of both spouses or civil partners is taken into account.

An article in Revenue Tax Bulletin August 2001 pp 876, 877, with worked example, illustrates how this rule, the no gain/no loss rule at **40.3** MARRIED PERSONS AND CIVIL PARTNERS and the matching rules at **58.2** SHARES AND SECURITIES generally interact.

As regards assets other than shares and securities, the question of whether the asset was a business asset (see **60.4** above) at any specified time in the combined period of holding is determined by reference to the use to which it was put by the spouse or civil partner holding it at that time. Thus, if a husband acquires a property on 1 April 1998 and holds it as an investment for four years after 5 April 1998 and then gives it to his wife who uses it in her business for five years before selling it, four-ninths of the gain on the ultimate disposal will attract nine years' taper relief at the non-business asset rate and five-ninths will attract nine years' taper relief at the business asset rate (see the rules at **60.12** above). During that part of the combined period of holding which falls *before* the inter-spouse or inter-partner transfer, the asset is also a business asset at any time if it then qualifies as such by reference to the spouse or civil partner to whom it is eventually transferred, i.e. where an asset owned by one spouse or partner is used in the other's business.

As regards shares and securities, the question of whether the asset was a business asset at any specified time in the combined period of holding is determined only by reference to the individual making the ultimate disposal. Say husband and wife each own 4% of the voting shares in a quoted trading company (acquired after 5 April 2000) but only the husband is an employee, and that this situation persists for five years at which point the wife gives her shareholding to her husband. After a further one year the husband sells the combined shareholding. The gain will attract six years' taper relief at the business asset rate, as the company has been a qualifying company by reference to the husband (see **60.6** above) throughout those six years. If, on the other hand, only the wife is an employee, only one-sixth of the ultimate gain will qualify for taper relief at the business asset rate. The company is a qualifying company by reference to the husband for only one of the six years; the fact that it is a qualifying company by reference to the wife for five of those years is irrelevant as it is not she who makes the ultimate disposal.

[*TCGA 1992, Sch A1 para 15; FA 1998, s 121(2)(4), Sch 20; FA 2003, s 160(4); SI 2005 No 3229, Reg 123*].'

63   Underwriters at Lloyd's

63.3   **Scottish limited partnerships and limited liability partnerships.** The text is amended to read as follows.

'Regulations provide for the tax treatment of profits or losses arising to the partners of a Scottish limited partnership or a limited liability partnership from its business as a Lloyd's underwriting member. They apply to accounting periods of Scottish limited partnerships ending on or after 1 December 1997 and to accounting periods of limited liability partnerships ending on or after 14 February 2006. See *SI 1997 No 2681* as amended by *SI 2006 No 111*.'

---

64   Unit Trusts, Investment Trusts and Open-Ended Investment Companies

---

64.3   **Investment trusts.** The following paragraph is added at the end.

'The Government intends to introduce legislation in the 2006 Finance Bill to enable the creation of real estate investment trusts in the UK. Draft legislation was published on the HMRC website on 14 December 2005.'

---

65   Venture Capital Trusts

65.8   **Withdrawal of relief on investment.** The first two paragraphs are amended to read as follows.

'*Disposal of investment.* Where an individual disposes of eligible shares, in respect of which relief has been claimed as under **65.7** above, within three years of their issue (five years for shares issued before 6 April 2000) and other than to a spouse or civil partner when they are living together (see below), then:

(*a*)   if the disposal is otherwise than at arm's length, relief given by reference to those shares is withdrawn;

(*b*)   if the disposal is at arm's length, the relief given by reference to those shares is reduced by an amount equivalent to tax at the appropriate rate (for the year for which relief was given) on the consideration received for the disposal (or withdrawn if the relief exceeds that amount). In relation to shares issued after 5 April 2004 and before 6 April 2006, the appropriate rate is the higher rate (currently 40%); in relation to shares issued before 6 April 2004 and after 5 April 2006, it is the lower rate (currently 20%).

Relief is **not** withdrawn where the disposal is by one spouse or civil partner to the other at a time when they are living together. However, on any subsequent disposal the spouse or partner to whom the shares were transferred is treated as if he or she were the person who subscribed for the shares, as if the shares had been issued to him or her at the time they were issued to the transferor spouse or partner, and as if his or her liability to income tax had been reduced by reference to those shares by the same amount, and for the same year of assessment, as applied on the subscription by the transferor spouse or partner. Any assessment for reducing or withdrawing relief is made on the transferee spouse or partner.'

In the list of statutory references immediately before the example, a reference to *SI 2005 No 3229, Reg 102* is added.

65.10   **Capital gains tax reliefs.** In the list of statutory references after the heading, a reference to *SI 2005 No 3229, Reg 128* is added.

65.12   **Deferral relief on reinvestment.** The list (A) to (H) is amended to read as follows.

'(A)   the investor disposes of the shares in his qualifying investment ('the relevant shares') otherwise than under *TCGA 1992, s 58* (a transfer between spouses or civil partners);

(B)   the relevant shares are disposed of by the spouse or civil partner of the investor (otherwise than by a transfer back to him), the spouse or partner having first acquired them from the investor under *TCGA 1992, s 58*;

(C) where shares falling within **65.11(3)** above are exchanged or treated as exchanged for any non-VCT holdings and under *TCGA 1992, s 135* or *TCGA 1992, s 136* (see **57.4** and **57.6** SHARES AND SECURITIES above) there is a requirement (or, but for *TCGA 1992, s 116* (see **48** QUALIFYING CORPORATE BONDS above) there would be a requirement) for those holdings to be regarded as the same assets as those shares;

(D) the investor becomes neither resident nor ordinarily resident in the UK whilst holding the relevant shares and within three years of the making of the qualifying investment (five years as regards shares issued before 6 April 2000);

(E) an individual who acquired the relevant shares through a transfer under *TCGA 1992, s 58* becomes neither resident nor ordinarily resident in the UK whilst holding those shares and within the period referred to in (D) above;

(F) the company in which the relevant shares are held has its approval as a VCT withdrawn (in a case in which approval is not treated as never having been given) (see **65.2** above);

(G) the relief given under **65.7** above by reference to relevant shares is withdrawn or reduced in circumstances not falling within (A)–(F) above;

(H) the 'prescribed winding-up period' of a VCT-in-liquidation comes to an end, the VCT-in-liquidation then still being in existence (see **65.2**(IV) above).'

In the list of statutory references before the example, a reference is added to *SI 2005 No 3229, Reg 128.*

---

68   Tax Case Digest

The following case is added.

Smallwood v HMRC 16.5

Losses on disposal of units in enterprise zone unit trust—whether TCGA 1992, s 41(2) applicable.

In 1989 an individual (S) invested £10,000 in an enterprise zone unit trust. The trustees used the funds to acquire land and buildings, and claimed capital allowances. S was credited with some of these allowances under *Income Tax (Definition of Unit Trusts Schemes) Regulations 1998 (SI 1998 No 267)*. Subsequently the property was disposed of and S received distributions, which were treated for CGT purposes as part disposals of S's units. S claimed that these disposals gave rise to allowable losses. The Revenue rejected the claim on the basis that the effect of *TCGA 1992, s 41(2)* was that S's allowable expenditure had to be restricted by the capital allowances. S appealed, contending that *section 41(2)* did not apply because it was the trustees' expenditure, rather than his expenditure, which gave rise to capital allowances. The Special Commissioner accepted this contention and allowed S's appeal, holding that 'once the step has been taken of treating the unit trust as a company and the rights of the unitholders as shares in that company, then for CGT purposes . . . the computation of gains on disposals of units must be treated in the same way as the computation of gains on disposals of shares'. Accordingly, the expression 'any expenditure to the extent to which any capital allowance ... has been or may be made in respect of it' in *TCGA 1992, s 41(2)* had to be construed as 'referring to expenditure comprised in the consideration given wholly and exclusively for the acquisition of the relevant asset, i.e. the £10,000 given by (S) for his units. Capital allowances were not given in respect of that expenditure. Thus *section 41(2)* does not apply.' *Smallwood v HMRC, Sp C 2005 (Sp C 509), [2006] SSCD 12.*

Budget Summary 22 March 2006

Note: It must be remembered that these proposals are subject to amendment during the passage of the Finance Bill.

PERSONAL TAXATION	2006/07	2005/06
Personal allowance		
general	£5,035	£4,895
aged 65 or over in year		
of assessment	£7,280	£7,090
aged 75 or over in year		
of assessment	£7,420	£7,220
age allowance income limit	£20,100	£19,500
minimum where income		
exceeds limit	£5,035	£4,895
Married couple's allowance		
(10% relief)		
either partner born before		
6 April 1935	£6,065	£5,905
either partner aged 75 or		
over in year of		
assessment	£6,135	£5,975
age allowance income limit	£20,100	£19,500
minimum where income		
exceeds limit	£2,350	£2,280
Blind person's allowance	£1,660	£1,610
Income tax rates		
Starting rate	10%	10%
on taxable income up to	£2,150	£2,090
Basic rate	22%	22%
on taxable income from		
starting rate limit up to	£33,300	£32,400
Higher rate	40%	40%
on taxable income over	£33,300	£32,400
Lower rate		
on certain interest income	20%	20%
Lower rate		
on dividend income	10%	10%
Higher rate		
on dividend income	32.5%	32.5%

COMPANY TAXATION	FY2006	FY2005
Corporation tax rates		
All companies (except below)	30%	30%
Companies with small profits	19%	19%
— 19% rate limit	£300,000	£300,000
— marginal relief limit	£1,500,000	£1,500,000
— marginal relief fraction	11/400	11/400
— marginal rate	32.75%	32.75%
Starting rate	N/A	0%
— 0% rate limit	N/A	£10,000
— marginal relief limit	N/A	£50,000
— marginal relief fraction	N/A	19/400
— marginal rate	N/A	23.75%
Non-corporate distribution rate	N/A	19%

CAPITAL GAINS TAX	2006/07	2005/06
Rate — general	10%*:20%*:40%*	10%*:20%*:40%*
— trustees and personal		
representatives	40%*	40%*
General exemption limit	£8,800	£8,500
*subject to taper relief where available		

INHERITANCE TAX	Transfers after 5/4/2006
Threshold	£285,000
(previously £275,000 for transfers after 5 April 2005)	
Death rate	40%

VAT	
Standard rate	17.5%
Registration threshold after 31 March 2006	£61,000
(previously £60,000 after 31 March 2005)	

NATIONAL INSURANCE	2006/07

(2005/06 in brackets where different)

Class 1 contributions

Not contracted out
The employee contribution is 11% of earnings between £97 (£94) and £645 (£630) p.w. plus 1% of all earnings above £645 (£630) p.w. The employer contribution is 12.8% of all earnings in excess of the first £97 (£94) p.w.

Contracted out
The 'not contracted out' rates for employees are reduced on the band of earnings from £97 (£94) p.w. to £645 (£630) p.w. by 1.6%. For employers, they are reduced on the band of earnings from £97 (£94) p.w. to £645 (£630) p.w. by 3.5% for employees in salary-related schemes or 1.0% for employees in money purchase schemes. In addition, there is an employee rebate of 1.6% and an employer rebate of 3.5% or 1.0%, as appropriate, on earnings from £84 (£82) p.w. up to £97 (£94) p.w.

Class 1A and 1B contributions		12.8%
Class 2 contributions		
Flat weekly rate	£2.10	(£2.10)
Exemption limit	£4,465	(£4,345)
Class 3 contributions		
Flat weekly rate	£7.55	(£7.35)

Class 4 contributions
8% on the band of profits between £5,035 (£4,895) and £33,540 (£32,760) *plus* 1% on all profits above £33,540 (£32,760).

PERSONAL TAX

Income Tax Rates and Allowances

For 2006/07, the lower, basic and higher rates of income tax remain at 10%, 22% and 40% respectively.

The starting rate band is increased by £60 to £2,150, and the basic rate band by £840 to £31,150 (so that the higher rate applies to taxable income in excess of £33,300).

The special rates applicable to dividends and other savings income are unchanged.

The rate applicable to discretionary and accumulation trusts remains at 40% (32.5% for dividend income). The 'basic rate' band for such trusts is increased from £500 to £1,000.

The basic personal allowance is increased by £140 to £5,035. For this and other personal reliefs, see the table on the previous page.

Dormant Accounts of Holocaust Victims

Certain compensation payments made in the year 1996/97 or any later year of assessment to holocaust victims and their heirs in relation to dormant accounts will be exempt from tax.

The measure exempts payments made by foreign banks and building societies, particularly under the Restore UK initiative or the Claims Resolution Tribunal arrangements for dormant accounts in Switzerland, and will cover both the interest that should have credited to the account and also revaluation of the original balance to take account of inflation. The exemption covers income tax, CGT on any gain arising from the disposal of a right to receive the payments and any additional IHT or earlier taxes which may have arisen to an estate from the rights to an original bank account immediately prior to the inception of the scheme concerned.

To qualify for the exemption the original account holder must be a 'victim of National-Socialist persecution'.

EMPLOYMENT TAX

Company Car and Fuel Benefits

The tax benefit of fuel provided for a company car is computed by applying to a set figure the percentage used in calculating the company car benefit itself. For 2006/07, that set figure is frozen at £14,400.

In computing the company car benefit, the lower carbon dioxide emissions threshold had already been frozen at 140g/km for 2006/07 and 2007/08. For 2008/09, it will be reduced to 135g/km. Cars with emissions of no more than the lower threshold qualify for the lowest rate (currently 15%) that can be applied to the list price of the car. However, for 2008/09, a new lower rate of 10% will be introduced for cars with carbon dioxide emissions of no more than 120g/km.

Exemptions for Computers and Mobile Phones

At present, where a computer is loaned by an employer to an employee for private use, the first £500 of the annual benefit in kind is exempt from income tax. This exemption is removed for 2006/07 onwards.

There is currently no limit on the number (or value) of mobile phones that can be loaned by an employer to an employee for private use. For 2006/07 onwards, the number of mobile phones that can be loaned without giving rise to a taxable benefit in kind is restricted to one per employee; there will be no exemption for phones loaned to a member of the employee's family or household. Also for 2006/07 onwards, if an employee receives a mobile phone under salary sacrifice arrangements, this will not give rise to a charge to tax on general earnings, even if the employee can surrender the phone for additional salary. If a voucher is used as a means of making a mobile phone available to an employee for private use, no charge to tax or NICs will arise if the benefit would have been exempt (i.e. under the one phone per employee rule above) if a voucher had not been used.

VDU Users: Eye Tests and Glasses

The legislation is amended to ensure that with effect from 6 April 2006 there will be no charge to an employee where his employer provides for him, or meets the cost of, eyecare tests and/or corrective glasses for VDU use. No charge will be made however the employer makes payment, whether it be by direct payment to the provider, reimbursement to the employee or by provision of a voucher to the employee. Currently, some non-cash vouchers are taxable.

Anti-avoidance: Employment-Related Securities

The Government announced on 2 December 2004 that any future legislation required to tackle tax and NICs avoidance in this area might be applied with retrospective effect from that date. Such retrospective legislation will now be included in *Finance Act 2006* to counter certain avoidance schemes that exploit the rules relating to options over shares and securities. The legislation will consist of a targeted purpose test to be applied where such an option is used as part of an avoidance scheme.

The option itself will be brought within the definition of a security, with the result that it may then be a convertible security to which pre-existing anti-avoidance legislation will apply. Draft legislation is available at www.hmrc.gov.uk/budget2006/ers-anti-avoidance.pdf and www.hmrc.gov.uk/budget2006/ers-paye.pdf.

Employer-supported Childcare

From 6 April 2006, the income tax and NICs exemption for employer-supported childcare is increased from £50 to £55 per week.

BUSINESS TAX

First-year Capital Allowances for Small Businesses

The rate of first-year allowance for expenditure on plant and machinery by small businesses (i.e. those already classed as 'small enterprises' for capital allowances purposes) is increased from 40% to 50% for one year only. The increased rate will apply to expenditure in the tax year 2006/07 for income tax purposes or in the 12 months from 1 April 2006 for corporation tax purposes. The rate for expenditure by medium-sized enterprises remains at 40%. Broadly, a 'small enterprise' is one which satisfies at least two of the following three conditions: turnover not exceeding £5.6 million, assets not exceeding £2.8 million, number of employees not exceeding 50.

Leased Plant and Machinery

As previously announced, the tax treatment of leased plant and machinery is to be brought into line with the treatment of plant and machinery acquired using other forms of finance. The new rules will apply to longer leases, to be known as 'long funding leases', which are essentially financing transactions. Leases of less than five years and, where certain conditions are met, of between five and seven years are generally excluded. Lessors will be able to make an election for the provisions to apply to certain leases which would otherwise be excluded where the value of the lease does not exceed £10 million. Special rules will apply to leases of ships to companies within the tonnage tax regime.

Where a lease falls within the provisions, the lessor will not be able to claim capital allowances and will be taxed only on the proportion of rentals that reflects the financing charges. The lessee will be able to claim capital allowances on an amount similar to that which would have applied had they bought the asset and will be able to obtain a deduction for that part of the rentals on which such allowances are not available.

The new provisions will apply, subject to transitional rules, to leases finalised on or after 1 April 2006.

In addition to these changes, minor amendments are to be made to the legislation applying to first-year allowances for lessors, plant and machinery acquired using hire purchase and certain finance costs incurred by companies carrying on oil extraction activities.

Landlords' Energy Saving Allowance

Landlords who pay income tax may already claim a deduction (the Landlords' Energy Saving Allowance (LESA)) against profits for expenditure to install loft insulation, cavity wall insulation or solid wall insulation in a dwelling house which they let. The maximum amount which may be claimed is limited to £1,500 per building.

With effect from 6 April 2006, the scope of the allowance is extended to include draught proofing and insulation for hot water systems.

CORPORATION TAX

Corporation Tax Rates

From 1 April 2006, the 0% starting rate and the 19% non-corporate distribution rate of tax are to be abolished. The current small companies rate of 19% and full rate of 30% will not be changed nor will there be any changes to the profit limits or marginal relief fractions.

Research and Development Tax Credits

It is proposed that from 1 April 2006, tax relief for qualifying expenditure will be extended to include payments made to clinical trial volunteers. In the case of the SME R&D scheme and vaccines research relief, which are notified state aids, the extension is subject to approval by the EC and will operate from a date to be appointed by Treasury Order.

The time limit for making claims for the enhanced deductions (or amendments or withdrawals) is to be changed to one year after the filing date for the tax return (currently six years after the end of the relevant accounting period). Claims relating to accounting periods ending before 31 March 2006, will need to be made by the earlier of the current time limit and 31 March 2008. This aligns the time limits for claims for enhanced deductions with those for payable credits.

Group Relief

In response to the ECJ judgment in the case of *Marks & Spencer plc v Halsey*, it is proposed that the UK group relief rules are extended to reflect EC law. The new relief will be available from 1 April 2006 to UK groups with foreign subsidiaries (including indirectly held subsidiaries) which have incurred foreign tax losses that cannot be relieved in the home state (or elsewhere) where those subsidiaries are either resident in the European Economic Area (EEA) or have incurred the relevant losses in a permanent establishment in the EEA. Relief will only be available for the foreign losses or other amounts that may be surrendered, computed under current UK tax rules. No relief will be given for amounts that represent a relieved foreign tax loss.

Measures will also be introduced, with effect from 20 February 2006, to deny loss relief when groups make arrangements one of the main purposes of which is to obtain UK relief where the arrangements either:

●   result in losses becoming unrelievable outside the UK that might otherwise be relievable; or

●   give rise to unrelievable losses which would not have arisen but for the availability of relief in the UK.

Securitisation and International Accounting Standards

A temporary tax regime for securitisation companies was introduced by *Finance Act 2005*, to enable such companies to be taxed on the basis of accounting standards in force before the introduction of International Accounting Standards. This regime was due to end on 31 December 2006, but in order to allow more time to develop a more permanent tax regime for securitisation companies, it is being extended to 31 December 2007. Amendments are also being made to the definitions of 'securitisation companies' for the purpose of the temporary regime, to ensure that it works as intended. Firstly, companies that issue debt in circumstances other than a securitisation will be excluded from the regime. However, companies which were within the regime on 22 March 2006, or were legally committed to entering into arrangements that would have brought them within the regime, can elect to retain the original rule. Other changes to the regime allow the inclusion of chains of intermediate borrowing companies, and extend the range of permitted activities that a note-issuing company can carry on so as to include the activity of acting as a guarantor.

Sale of Lessors

Where the economic ownership of a company carrying on a business of leasing plant or machinery changes hands after 4 December 2005, it is proposed that a tax charge is imposed on the lessor company on the date of the sale and an equal and opposite relief granted to the lessor company on the day after the sale. The charge would apply in respect of long leases where in the early years of a lease the capital allowances available to the lessor company are greater than the rental income from the lease, giving rise to losses. The charge would broadly equate to the tax benefit of such losses. This is to prevent the lessor company making use of such losses to defer (sometimes indefinitely) the tax on the leasing profits. For example, the losses can be surrendered as group relief and the profits arising in the later years of the lease (when the rental income is greater than the capital allowances) can be sheltered on the sale of the lessor company to a group with tax losses. The charge would thus counter the losses available to the original owner and the corresponding relief would counter the profits passed on to the new owner.

There are provisions to account for partial sales and the measure covers leasing businesses carried on in a consortium and through a partnership. It also covers the deferral of profits sheltered from tax through unusual partnership profit-sharing arrangements, the non-arm's length transfer of assets between parties and transactions whereby on the sale of a leased asset, the vendor retains all or part of the rental income.

This proposal was published on 5 December 2005 but is to be amended to reflect developments in the reform of the taxation of leasing and comments following the publication of draft legislation. Any beneficial changes (reducing the scope or effect of the measure) will have effect from 5 December 2005; other changes will have effect from 22 March 2006.

Controlled Foreign Companies

Where a company is resident both in the UK and, under double taxation relief arrangements, in a territory outside the UK, it is treated by *FA 1994, s 249* as resident outside the UK. However, under *ICTA 1988, s 747(1B)*, where companies became non-resident from 1 April 2002 for other tax purposes, *s 249* is disregarded in determining whether a company is UK resident for the purposes of the CFC legislation. It is proposed that from 22 March 2006, this provision will also apply to companies which became non-resident as a result of a double tax treaty before 1 April 2002 so that such companies cannot be used for tax avoidance.

Corporate Capital Losses

As previously announced, anti-avoidance rules are to be introduced to restrict the creation and use of capital losses by companies to genuine commercial transactions. The rules apply from 5 December 2005 and are intended to deter:

- contrived creation of capital losses;
- buying of capital gains and losses; and
- conversion of income streams into capital gains, or creation of capital gains matched by income deductions, where the gains are then wholly or partly covered by allowable losses.

Financial Products Avoidance

The *2006 Finance Bill* will block a number of avoidance schemes notified to HMRC under the *Finance Act 2004* disclosure rules.

Budget Summary

They involve financial products designed to avoid tax including many intra-group arrangements to avoid tax on income arising within the group or create a tax loss when there is no loss to the group as a whole.

Film Tax Relief

A new relief will be available for British films intended for cinema exhibition, starting production on or after 1 April 2006. To be eligible, qualifying UK expenditure must be at least 25% of total production expenditure on the film.

British films will be as defined by revisions to the *Films Act 1985*. Qualifying UK expenditure must be directly incurred in relation to production, principal photography and post-production activities taking place within the UK. (Other film-related expenditure will be subject to normal tax rules.)

There will also be new treatment for film production companies (FPCs), defined for tax purposes as a company responsible for principal photography, post-production and delivering the completed film. Each film will be treated as a separate trade.

There will be an additional tax deduction for UK production expenditure of:

● 100% for films with total qualifying production expenditure of £20m or less; and

● 80% for all other films.

Where this gives rise to a loss, this can be surrendered for a tax credit calculated at 25% for qualifying expenditure up to £20m and 20% for other films. Alternatively it can be carried forward and set against future income.

The existing relief will continue to apply to qualifying films where principal photography started by 31 March 2006 and is completed by 1 January 2007 or acquisition expenditure where acquisition takes place before 1 October 2007.

CAPITAL GAINS

Bed and Breakfasting

Measures have been introduced to counter tax avoidance schemes which exploit the bed and breakfasting rules in certain circumstances to ensure that no CGT is payable on substantial gains.

The bed and breakfasting rules set out in *TCGA 1992, s 106A* are part of the identification rules which apply on the disposal of securities and are designed to prevent those within the charge to CGT disposing of securities and acquiring identical ones shortly afterwards for the purpose of realising a tax-free capital gain or a capital loss while still, in effect, holding on to the investment.

The amendment prevents the rules applying in relation to acquisitions made at times when the person making the disposal:

● is neither resident nor ordinarily resident in the UK; or

● is resident or ordinarily resident in the UK, but is 'treaty non-resident', i.e. is regarded as resident in a territory which is outside the UK for tax treaty purposes.

Where the amendment has effect, the gain or loss on the disposal will be calculated on the basis that the securities disposed of were acquired before the disposal, rather than being those acquired within 30 days of the disposal.

The change will apply in relation to acquisitions made on or after 22 March 2006, irrespective of when the disposal was made.

SAVINGS AND INVESTMENTS

New Pensions Regime from 6 April 2006 (A-Day)

The new regime has already been legislated for in *Finance Acts 2004* and *2005* and numerous regulations made by statutory instrument, and is well-publicised. Additional measures are to be included in *Finance Act 2006*. These had already been announced prior to Budget Day (see, for example, the Pre-Budget Report on 5 December 2005 and www.hmrc.gov.uk/pensionschemes/pts-measures.htm) and include the following 'anti-abuse' measures:

- the removal of tax advantages for self-directed pension schemes of investing in residential property and in assets such as fine wines, classic cars and antiques;

- measures to deter the artificial boosting of pension funds by the recycling of tax-free lump sums (see www.hmrc.gov.uk/budget2006/recycling.pdf for latest draft legislation).

UK Real Estate Investment Trusts

With effect from 1 January 2007, companies and groups of companies whose main business is property investment, and who meet the necessary conditions, will be able to elect for special rules to apply to their property business and to their distributions. Those that elect will be known as UK-REITs (real estate investment trusts). Qualifying rental income and gains made on the disposal of investment property will be exempt from corporation tax and dividends paid, to the extent that they relate to tax-exempt profits, will be treated for UK tax purposes as income from property and will be paid under deduction of tax.

Profits and gains on any other activity carried on by the REIT will be subject to corporation tax in the normal way and dividends paid out of other profits will be treated as normal dividends for UK tax purposes.

To come within the UK-REIT regime, at least 90% of the company's tax-exempt profits must be distributed each year and, in addition, various other conditions must be met.

With regard to the company:

- it must be UK resident for tax purposes;

- its shares must be listed on a recognised stock exchange; and

- no one investor may be beneficially entitled to 10% or more of the distributions or control directly or indirectly 10% or more of the share capital or voting rights.

The conditions that relate to the business are that:

- 75% or more of its assets must be investment property;

- 75% or more of its income must be rental income; and

- the ratio of interest on loans to fund the tax-exempt business to rental income of that business must be less than 1.25:1.

Companies or groups wanting to become REITs must pay an entry charge of 2% of the market value of their investment properties at the date they join the scheme. This charge will be collected at the same time as any corporation tax due for the first accounting period to which the scheme applies or by instalments over four years if the company so applies.

The legislation relating to housing investment trusts (*ICTA 1988, ss 508A–508B*) will be repealed at the same time as REITs come into force.

Venture Capital Schemes

The rate of income tax relief for investors in venture capital trusts (VCTs) is decreased from 40% to 30% in relation to shares issued on or after 6 April 2006, and the minimum period for which investors must retain the shares is increased from three years to five in relation to such shares. At present, a VCT is required to have 70% by value of its investments represented by shares or securities in qualifying holdings and can have no more than 15% of its total investments in any one company; from 6 April 2007, any money held by a VCT or on its behalf will be treated as an investment for the purposes of these tests. There is a significant change to the 'gross assets' test, which determines the size of company a VCT may invest in; in relation to investment of funds raised after 5 April 2006, the relevant assets of the investee company must not exceed £7 million immediately before the investment and £8 million immediately afterwards. These limits were previously £15 million and £16 million respectively.

Relief is currently available under the enterprise investment scheme (EIS) on investment of up to £200,000 per tax year. With effect for shares issued on or after 6 April 2006, this limit is increased to £400,000. The amount that may be carried back to the previous tax year is similarly increased from £25,000 to £50,000. The above changes to the 'gross assets' test apply also for EIS purposes; they apply to shares issued on or after 6 April 2006 unless they were subscribed for before 22 March 2006. As regards investments made by approved investment funds, the changes to the test will not apply if the Fund was approved before 22 March 2006 and raising money before 6 April 2006.

The above changes to the 'gross assets' test apply also to the corporate venturing scheme (CVS); they apply to shares issued on or after 6 April 2006 unless they were subscribed for before 22 March 2006.

Alternative Finance Arrangements

Finance Act 2005 introduced legislation to deal with finance arrangements that are structured so that they do not involve the payment or receipt of interest. It enabled certain financial arrangements to be taxed in a manner similar to those involving interest but which do not go counter to Islamic law prohibitions. It also ensured that other rules relating to interest, such as deduction of tax at source, apply in the same way as other finance arrangements.

New provisions will amend and build on *FA 2005* by providing for two additional alternative finance arrangements to be taxed on a level playing field to products involving interest. These provisions relate to an agency-style contract, which is equivalent to a saving account, and a partnership-style arrangement used to finance the purchase of property or other assets. This will be achieved by providing that, where certain conditions are met, amounts equating economically to interest that are paid by the financial institution to the investor, or received by the financial institution, are to be charged to tax on the same basis as interest.

In addition, the proposed revision also amends *FA 2005* to provide that low cost alternative finance arrangements provided by employers to employees are treated in the same way as conventional low-interest loans to employees, where existing legislation provides that a taxable benefit in kind arises from a 'taxable cheap loan' made to an employee. The difference between the amount of interest actually payable, and the amount of interest that would be payable at the official rate, represents the taxable benefit.

The provision relating to alternative finance arrangements made available to employees will apply to arrangements entered into on or after 22 March 2006. The remaining provisions apply to arrangements entered into on or after 6 April 2006 for income tax purposes and 1 April 2006 for corporation tax purposes.

INHERITANCE TAX

Inheritance Tax Thresholds

The nil-rate band for 2006/07 is £285,000. In addition, the thresholds above which the nil-rate band ceases to apply for future years have been set at £300,000 for 2007/08, £312,000 for 2008/09 and £325,000 for 2009/10.

Aligning the Inheritance Tax Treatment of Trusts

Changes are to be made to the special inheritance tax rules applying to accumulation and maintenance (A&M) and interest in possession (IIP) trusts. Legislation in the forthcoming *Finance Bill* will limit the rules to trusts that are created:

- on death by a parent for a minor child who will be fully entitled to the assets in the trust at age 18;

- on death for the benefit of one life tenant in order of time whose interest cannot be replaced (more than one such trust may be created on death as long as the trust capital vests absolutely when the life interest comes to an end); or

- either in the settlor's lifetime or on death for a disabled person.

Any other trusts will fall into the mainstream IHT rules for 'relevant property' trusts, broadly those trusts in which no person has an interest in possession. Changes to the IHT treatment of trusts will have a number of implications for capital gains tax particularly in relation to hold-over relief.

The new rules will apply on and after 22 March 2006 to new trusts, additions of new assets to existing trusts and, subject to transitional provisions, to other IHT relevant events in relation to existing trusts. Transitional rules will provide for a period of adjustment for certain existing trusts up to 6 April 2008, and for continuing exclusion from the 'relevant property' charges if they satisfy certain conditions for ongoing protection.

Changes are also to be made to the inheritance tax gifts with reservation provisions. Where an individual is beneficially entitled to an interest in settled property, and continues to be treated for IHT purposes as owning the property, a termination of the interest in the individual's lifetime on or after 22 March 2006 will be treated as a gift for the purposes of the provisions. So if the individual retains the use of the settled property after their interest in it ends, it will remain chargeable in their hands in the same way as if the individual had formerly owned it outright.

Pensions Simplification and Inheritance Tax

IHT concessionary practice dating from 1992 in relation to pension choices by scheme members who die under the age of 75 is to be put on a statutory footing. Under the concession, IHT is not charged if scheme members do not exercise their right to take pension benefits, for example, when an enhanced death benefit is paid to a beneficiary who is a spouse, civil partner or financial dependant of the scheme member as a result of the member not taking their pension when their life expectancy was seriously impaired.

An anti-avoidance measure is to be introduced to charge IHT on the death on or after the age of 75 of a scheme member where funds are held in an alternatively secured pension (ASP). The charge is intended to apply in the case where individuals use ASPs to pass on tax-privileged retirement savings to their dependants rather than to provide a pension in retirement. Broadly, an IHT charge will be made on certain left-over ASP funds on death of the scheme member (or later) but funds paid to charity will be exempt. The charge will be based on the value of the taxable property at the time the charge arises and will be calculated by reference to the tax-free threshold and rate of tax in place at that time. The measure will also cover two instances where the tax charge on ASP funds overlap.

The above provisions are to take effect on the death of a scheme member after 5 April 2006.

CHARITIES

Income and Corporation Tax Relief for Trading Activities

For chargeable periods commencing after 21 March 2006, tax relief will be available for charities where only part of a trade is carried on for a primary (charitable) purpose or where a trade is partly (but not mainly) carried out by the beneficiaries of a charity. The new rules will legitimise the effect of the current

HMRC approach. It will split a trade into two separate parts, a primary purpose part and a non-primary purpose part, with tax relief under ICTA 1988, s 505 given on the profits of the primary purpose part or on the profits of the part carried out by the beneficiaries of the charity.

Anti-avoidance Provisions

New rules will be introduced to protect charitable reliefs from misuse.

(1)   After 21 March 2006, additional restrictions will be placed on transactions that can take place between a charity and its substantial donors without the charity's tax relief being restricted. An individual or a company will be a substantial donor if they give to a charity £25,000 or more in any 12-month period or £100,000 over a 6-year period. The donor will be a substantial donor for the chargeable period in which they exceed these limits and the following five chargeable periods. The new rules will apply to the sale or letting of property; the provision of services by a charity to a substantial donor or vice versa; an exchange of property between a charity and a substantial donor; the provision of financial assistance to a charity by a substantial donor or vice versa; the payment of remuneration to a substantial donor (apart from an approved payment for services as a trustee); and investment by a charity in the business of a substantial donor as long as the business is not listed on a recognised stock exchange. Certain transactions by a substantial donor to a charity will be exempt from the new rules if HMRC are satisfied that they are undertaken for genuine commercial reasons or at arm's length, provided the transaction is not part of an arrangement for the avoidance of tax. The new rules will not apply to a disposal at less than market value by a substantial donor to a charity to which *ICTA 1988, s 587B* (gifts of shares security and real property to charity, etc.) or *TCGA 1992, s 257* (gifts to charities, etc.) apply.

Where a charity takes part in any of the transactions that are not otherwise exempt, any payments it makes in connection with the transaction will be treated as non-charitable expenditure. Where the transaction is not on arm's length terms, any difference between the actual terms and arm's length terms, so far as it favours the substantial donor, will be treated as non-charitable expenditure.

(2)   In respect of non-charitable expenditure incurred in a chargeable period commencing after 21 March 2006, there will be a direct link between non-charitable expenditure incurred by a charity and loss of tax relief. The income and gains eligible for tax relief will be restricted by £1 for every £1 of non-charitable expenditure incurred.

(3)   For payments to charity made after 31 March 2006, non-close companies will be subject to the same limits on benefits received as a result of a gift to charity as currently apply for individuals and close companies. They will also become subject to the same rules as close companies and individuals that apply when gifts are potentially repayable or are associated with the acquisition of property by the charity from the donor or connected persons.

TRUSTS

Modernising the Tax System for Trusts

For 2006/07 onwards, the 'basic rate' band available to the trustees of discretionary trusts and accumulation and maintenance trusts is increased from £500 to £1,000.

Following an earlier consultation exercise, a number of definitions and tests used in taxing trusts to income tax and capital gains tax are to be altered and aligned across the two taxes. The main changes are:

- a common test as to whether trustees are UK-resident;

- a common meaning of 'settled property' and thus of 'settlement';

- a common meaning of 'settlor';

- provision for trustees to be treated as one person; and

- provision for trustees to elect that a sub-fund of the settlement be treated as a separate settlement in certain circumstances.

These changes have effect for 2006/07 onwards, apart from the first-listed change, which has effect for 2007/08 onwards. The new definitions and tests may not apply for all purposes, for example certain anti-avoidance purposes.

The following changes will also be introduced for 2006/07 onwards:

- the income of settlor-interested trusts is to be treated as though it had arisen directly to the settlor;

- an existing practice of not taxing beneficiaries in receipt of discretionary income from settlor-interested trusts is to be given statutory effect; and

- modifications will be made to certain pre-existing capital gains rules which determine whether a settlor has an interest in the settlement.

Some of the proposed changes included in the earlier consultation exercise, for example income streaming and changes to the capital gains taxation of deceased persons' estates, are not being taken forward at this time.

GENERAL ANTI-AVOIDANCE

Changes to the Disclosure Regime

With effect from 1 July 2006, the existing *Tax Avoidance Schemes (Prescribed Description of Arrangements) Regulations* will be revoked. New Regulations will apply to the whole of income tax, corporation tax and capital gains tax and contain hallmarks (descriptions of arrangements in line with the system already used for VAT). If a scheme falls within any one hallmark then it will be notifiable. The hallmarks will fall into three groups:

- three generic hallmarks that target new and innovative schemes (derived from the existing 'filters' of confidentiality, premium fee and off-market terms);

- a hallmark that targets mass marketed tax products; and

- hallmarks that target areas of particular risk.

Two specific hallmarks will concern schemes intended to create tax losses to offset income or capital gains tax and certain leasing schemes.

The time limit for disclosure of schemes devised in-house will be reduced to 30 days from the date that the scheme is implemented. But a de minimis provision will be added so that neither individuals nor businesses that are SMEs will have to disclose in-house schemes.

International Tax Enforcement Arrangements

New powers will allow the UK to enter into bilateral and multilateral arrangements for the exchange of information in relation to both direct and indirect taxes. The existing rules provide for arrangements only in respect of direct taxes. They will also provide for such arrangements to include, for the first time, provisions on mutual assistance in tax collection in respect of both direct and indirect taxes. The provisions will have effect from the date of Royal Assent to the *Finance Bill*.

STAMP TAXES

Residential Property Threshold

The threshold for stamp duty land tax (SDLT) on residential property has been raised from £120,000 to £125,000. As a result of this change, SDLT will not be charged on transactions in residential property if the chargeable consideration does not exceed £125,000. Tax will be payable at 1% where the consideration exceeds £125,000 but does not exceed £250,000. The change in threshold applies to transactions with an effective date on or after 23 March 2006. The effective date is normally the date of completion, not the date of exchange of contracts.

Simplification and Clarification of the Law

Finance Bill 2006 will introduce some measures to simplify and clarify various aspects of SDLT. These measures will take effect on Royal Assent. In addition, regulations have been made which will take certain transactions outside the scope of SDLT. These have effect from 12 April 2006.

The regulations will deem that the following features of common land transactions are not chargeable consideration:

●   a gift of property on which the donee or beneficiary agrees, or is required, to pay any capital gains tax or inheritance tax arising;

●   the payment of a landlord's reasonable costs on the grant, variation or termination of a lease; and

●   a covenant by an agricultural tenant to assign entitlement to the Single Farm Payment to the landlord on termination of the tenancy.

The measures to be introduced by *Finance Bill 2006* will:

●   remove the SDLT charge on a transfer of an interest in a partnership whose main activity is the carrying on of a trade (other than a trade of dealing in or developing land) or a profession;

●   remove a potential double charge on partnerships;

●   clarify the rules on 'successive linked leases' in cases where an agreement for lease is followed by the grant of a lease;

●   simplify the rules on variations in rent;

●   clarify the treatment of rent reviews in the case of agricultural tenancies, as well as the treatment of 'interim rents' in the case of business tenancies;

●   simplify the treatment of 'backdated' leases which are expressed to commence immediately after the expiry of a former lease;

●   clarify the rules on notifying assignments of leases; and

●   ensure that no SDLT charge applies to transfers of assets between sub-funds of a settlement.

Withdrawal of Unit Trust 'Seeding Relief'

HMRC have announced the withdrawal of the exemption from SDLT that applied when property was transferred into a newly formed unit trust in consideration for the issue of units. The withdrawal of 'seeding relief' takes effect for all transfers into unit trusts on or after 22 March 2006, although there are transitional arrangements for contracts entered into before 2 p.m. on that date. As a result of the withdrawal of 'seeding relief', the general rules on chargeable consideration apply so that the consideration for the issue of units is the market value of the property transferred. FA 2003, s 53, which deems the chargeable consideration to be no less than market value where the transaction involves a connected company, is extended to transfers to trustees of a unit trust scheme. However, there are two circumstances in which that section does not apply. The first is where the transfer is effected in pursuance of a contract entered into and substantially performed before 2 p.m. on 22 March 2006. The second is where the transfer is in pursuance of any other contract entered into before that time, provided that the transfer to the trustees is not 'an excluded transaction'. This is an anti-avoidance measure. The definition of 'excluded transaction' is drafted so as to preclude attempts to obtain 'seeding relief' by varying contracts, and assigning rights in contracts, existing before 2 p.m. on 22 March 2006.

Extension of Alternative Finance Reliefs

There will be an extension of the reliefs currently available to individuals who purchase land and buildings using alternative financing arrangements. Such arrangements are normally structured to preclude the payment of interest. Relief is given to ensure that the SDLT chargeable is no more than would be chargeable under more traditional loan finance arrangements. These reliefs are currently only available to individuals but, with effect from Royal Assent to *Finance Bill 2006*, they will be extended to all persons, so that companies, clubs and trusts can also take advantage of alternative financing arrangements.

Stamp Duty Reconstruction Reliefs

The rules governing relief from stamp duty for certain company reconstructions and acquisitions are to be amended. One of the conditions for relief is that the registered office of the acquiring company should be in the UK. This condition will be removed so that, provided the other conditions are met, the reliefs will be available to acquiring companies worldwide. Another condition for relief is that, after the acquisition has been made, there should be no change in the proportion of the company or its business that is owned by each shareholder. The rules will be amended so that the relief is preserved in cases where the proportion of shares held by each shareholder in the new structure has to change slightly for practical reasons. These changes take effect from Royal Assent to *Finance Bill 2006*.

VALUE ADDED TAX

Registration and Deregistration

With effect from 1 April 2006, the VAT registration threshold (the annual taxable turnover limit which determines whether a person must be registered for VAT) will be increased from £60,000 to £61,000. The deregistration threshold will be increased from £58,000 to £59,000. The registration and deregistration thresholds for acquisitions from other EU member states will also be increased from £60,000 to £61,000.

Car Fuel Scale Charges

The scale used to charge VAT on fuel used for private motoring in business cars will be increased from the start of the first VAT period beginning on or after 1 May 2006. The revised scale charges are as follows:

Annual returns

Cylinder capacity of vehicle	*Scale charge diesel* £	*VAT due per car* £	*Scale charge other* £	*VAT due per car* £
Up to 1,400 cc	1,040	154.89	1,095	163.09
1,401 cc to 2,000 cc	1,040	154.89	1,385	206.28
2,001 cc or more	1,325	197.34	2,035	303.09

Quarterly returns

Cylinder capacity of vehicle	*Scale charge diesel* £	*VAT due per car* £	*Scale charge other* £	*VAT due per car* £
Up to 1,400 cc	260	38.72	273	40.66
1,401 cc to 2,000 cc	260	38.72	346	51.53
2,001 cc or more	331	49.30	508	75.66

Budget Summary

Monthly returns

Cylinder capacity of vehicle	Scale charge diesel £	VAT due per car £	Scale charge other £	VAT due per car £
Up to 1,400 cc	86	12.81	91	13.55
1,401 cc to 2,000 cc	86	12.81	115	17.13
2,001 cc or more	110	16.38	169	25.17

Partial Exemption

An informal consultation will be held on two changes to strengthen and simplify the special method regime.

The first change would require a business to declare that its proposed special method is fair and reasonable before gaining approval for its use. HMRC could then set aside a method that the business should have known was not fair and reasonable in order to recoup VAT that has been incorrectly reclaimed.

The second change would simplify the rules for partly exempt businesses that make overseas supplies. HMRC would be able to approve a special method that deals with the recovery of VAT on costs that relate to supplies made outside the UK that confer the right of deduction (e.g. supplies of finance and insurance made to customers outside the EU).

The Government intends to introduce the changes from April 2007.

Powers Relating to the Inspection of Goods

With effect from Royal Assent to the *Finance Bill*, HMRC officers will have the right to mark (e.g. by applying an HMRC date stamp) any goods inspected, and to record details of the goods by any means (e.g. by electronic scanning of barcodes). The measure is a clarification of what HMRC consider their existing powers.

Power to Direct Additional Record-keeping Requirements

With effect from Royal Assent to the *Finance Bill*, HMRC will have the power to direct individual businesses to keep specified records relating to goods which they have traded. The power will only be used where HMRC have reasonable grounds to believe that the records may assist in the identification of supplies where VAT might go unpaid (e.g. supplies of mobile phones and computer chips).

Failure to comply with a direction will give rise to a penalty. Both the issue of a direction and the imposition of a penalty will be appealable matters.

Taxation of Face Value Vouchers

With effect from Royal Assent to the Finance Bill, two measures are to be introduced in relation to the taxation of face value vouchers.

The first measure relates to *VATA 1994, Sch 10A para 3(3)* (which provides that where VAT is not accounted for on goods and services which are obtained on the redemption of a credit voucher, the supply of the credit voucher becomes subject to VAT). New rules may be introduced by statutory instrument, specifying additional circumstances in which the voucher becomes subject to VAT.

The second measure will clarify the wording of *art 21* of the *VAT (Place of Supply of Services) Order, SI 1992/3121*. The current wording ('a right to services') is considered ambiguous, and it appears that the wording is to be amended to 'a right to receive services'.

Rewrite of VATA 1994, Sch 10 (Buildings and Land)

The Finance Act 2006 will introduce enabling legislation providing for the rewrite of *VATA 1994, Sch 10*. A Treasury Order will provide for a wholesale rewrite of the Schedule, including consequential, supplementary and transitional provisions and amendments. The amendments will include the granting of new appeal rights.

The enabling legislation will come into effect from the date of Royal Assent to the *Finance Bill*. The Treasury Order will be laid before Parliament shortly after that.

Person Responsible for Accounting and Payment on Sales of Certain Goods

A new *section 55A* to *VATA 1994* will provide that the purchaser, rather than the seller, must account for and pay the VAT due on the sale of specified goods (such as mobile phones, computer chips and some other similar electronic items).

The measure, which is intended to combat missing trader intra-community fraud, will also provide that the value of those goods is be included in the taxable turnover of the purchaser for VAT registration purposes.

Since bad debt relief will not apply, a consequential amendment will allow an adjustment of output tax where entitlement to input tax is disallowed under *VATA 1994, s 26A* (i.e. where payment has not been made within sixth months).

Secondary legislation will specify the goods to which the new section will apply, and any exceptions thereto.

The measure requires a derogation from the *EC Sixth Directive*; consequently it will come into force when other EU Member States have agreed to the proposal.

Supplies of Goods under Finance Agreements

Where goods are returned before an agreement is completed, finance companies will no longer be able to treat them as 'neither a supply of goods nor services' for VAT purposes when sold for a second time if VAT on the first sale can be adjusted. This will apply whether the goods are returned because the customer exercises their right to do so or the finance company exercises its rights because the customer defaults.

The change applies to all finance agreements entered into after 12 April 2006 where the goods concerned are delivered after 31 August 2006.

Auctioneers' Fees

Following a recent decision by the European Court of Justice, UK legislation will be changed to ensure that commission charged by an auctioneer will be taxed in the same way, irrespective of whether the auctioned goods are within temporary importation (TI) arrangements or are in free circulation within the EU. Currently, the buyer's premium in respect of goods auctioned within TI arrangements is taxed by including the commission in the valuation of the goods at final importation into the EU (i.e. at an effective reduced rate of VAT equal to 5%). Following the change, it will be taxed at 17.5%.

The revised provisions will take effect shortly after Royal Assent to the *Finance Bill*.

Reduced Rate – Contraceptives

The reduced rate of 5% is to apply to all sales of contraceptive products, other than those already zero-rated or supplied as part of an exempt supply of health care.

The operative date of the change is subject to Parliamentary approval but is expected to be 1 July 2006.

OLYMPIC GAMES

Olympics Tax Exemptions

In preparation for 2012, the London Organising Committee of the Olympic Games Ltd is to be exempted from corporation tax from incorporation (22 October 2004).

The Government also plans to ensure that International Olympic Committee revenues generated from the games and income of other persons temporarily in the UK to carry out Olympic-related business will also be exempt.